Praise for Inside Out Transformation

"The inside-out understanding is infinitely deeper and more helpful than any of the countless therapies and self-help techniques I've tried. I'm so grateful to have the leaders in this paradigm all together in one amazing book. It's a fabulous resource to share with the practitioners I work with!"

Amy Johnson, PhD, Three Principles Coach and Trainer, Author of *The Little Book of Big Change*

"It's truly an honour to review a book of such substance. This collection of gems from the first generation of Three Principles teachers will remain a classic in the field of innate health literature, no doubt in my mind. This book is a precious gift for us younger generations of sharers of this powerful understanding of the universal truths behind the human mind.

Sheela has worked her quiet magic behind the scenes while putting this book together – and you should never underestimate the power of quiet. In short, Sheela has written a book that blows my mind, about an understanding that will continue to blow my mind for the rest of my life."

Mette Louise Holland, Psychologist, Three Principles Trainer and Coach, Author of *Dit selvhelbredende Sind (Danish)*

"This is the first Three Principles book of its kind! It's like Sheela has done all the heavy lifting for us readers and given us a priceless gift for life. I love the way no two conversations are the same despite all the coaches and teachers pointing to the same truth. Sheela's down to earth style of posing questions from a place of love and understanding has led to some rich, refreshing and insightful conversations. Highly recommend this book!"

Dr Rani Bora, Holistic Psychiatrist, Wellness Coach and Author of *How to Turn Stress on its Head*

"This book is literally a goldmine, there are so many treasures in the form of insights, experience and wisdom to be had! Sheela has given us a sneak peek into the world of some of the best teachers of the Three Principles, letting us listen to them describe what they do and how they do it with humility, humour and grace. I feel like I went on a coaching course whilst reading this book, it is so rich with good things, I can't wait to read it again!"

Chana Studley, Three Principles Practitioner, Speaker, and Author of *Painless*

"I'm grateful to Sheela for bringing this much needed book into the world. I love the way the fundamentals of teaching from the Three Principles understanding has been laid out by the people who were directly impacted by Syd Banks, the source of the discovery. I love the way each teacher points to some simple truths we can all use in our practice. They are certainly what I've been using in my workshops in prisons. Inmates are people and when any person understands what they've been misunderstanding about how our experience is created and what they can rely on, we get to see transformative shifts in their consciousness and therefore their behaviour, their relationships and their ability to thrive."

Jaqueline B Hollows, Social Entrepreneur, International Speaker, Author of *A Different Story*

"I love this book. There I said it.

The author's idea is simple and brilliant: have a conversation with some of the people who learned directly from Syd Banks and ask them what insights they have gained over the years about working with clients and transformation.

I came to the Three Principles understanding in 2013 and my life was transformed in a relatively short period of time. I went from many years of deep anxiety and chronic depression to now, a lighter, richer, deeper, more engaged and meaningful experience of life. I quit my business and became a coach and mentor because I had been so impacted by what I had learned. I knew that I had to share it with the world. As I have coached, over the years, my own understanding has become deeper and simpler. As a result my life just unfolds with even more grace.

Thank you Sheela. I think this book will become required reading for anyone that wants to impact the world with their client work. No more, no less. Just saying."

Stef Cybichowski, Transformative Coach & Mentor

"This book beautifully points to that which is beyond any method or theory. It provides first hand accounts from the direct students of Sydney Banks on how they work with clients from a Principles based understanding. The book reveals how understanding the inside-out nature of experience has tremendous transformational power on people from all walks of life, and is a gift for anyone who wants to improve their coaching, therapy or counselling! I highly recommend reading this incredible source of wisdom".

Natasha Swerdloff, Co-author of *Coming Home: Uncovering the Foundations of Psychological Wellbeing*

"In her new book, *Inside Out Transformation*, Sheela has achieved a remarkable feat. She has diligently documented the insights of 15 of the most impactful change workers on the planet! This book is important. Not only does it spotlight a beautiful possibility for each one of us, it also shares valuable experiences we can all learn from. I believe it will become required reading for all coaches and therapists who work with an understanding of the Three Principles."

Thomas Leamy, Psychology and Performance Consultant, Coach and Trainer, High Performance Strategy Europe (HPSE)

"The inside-out transformation is a 180 degree shift in where we point to the answers that will help our clients have a transformative experience. Once they gain insight, their experience of life will naturally become more joyful, and they will experience peace of mind.

What Sheela illustrates throughout the book is the true nature of all human beings, beyond the psychological concepts we learn in traditional western theories of psychology, to simple spiritual facts.

The teachers featured in this book have been instrumental in facilitating transformational experiences for thousands, if not tens of thousands of people including my own. This understanding has been life-changing for me – after 40 years of addiction, psychiatric diagnoses, and eating disorders, I was free after a momentary realisation."

Jason Shiers, Certified Psychotherapist, Coach and Author

"There is something very ordinary in the beautiful simplicity that emerges from this book. And yet at the same time it is extra-ordinary, not least because the pages of *Inside Out Transformation* contain the potential to impact every reader with a deeper peace of mind and sense of clarity both in their own experience of life and in serving another as a coach/therapist/counsellor.

Whether a veteran or newbie, there is something for everyone. It is impossible not to fall more deeply in love with the purity and power of this inside-out paradigm based on the teachings of Sydney Banks. One of the many gifts in this book is the quiet, grounded certainty that it invokes in the reader. In their own unique voices, each of the 15 renowned leaders remind us clearly of the only essentials at play here, namely a willingness to listen deeply from a state of love and presence, seeing the wellbeing of our clients, and an openness to follow what shows up in this space. I know that I will be referring to this magical guide time and time again!"

Carina Loweth, Transformative Coach

"I can only describe Sheela's meticulously researched book as 'The Who's Who of The Three Principles'.

In it she describes the fascinating ideas of some of these best-known Three Principles mental health professionals. These are the people who knew and learned from Sydney Banks personally and got involved in the very early days.

In Sheela's insightful book, she walks us through how these brilliant practitioners are able to help their clients to see something special and new about how we experience our lives here on earth.

It is a really valuable contribution to the Three Principles."

John Doorbar, Trainer, Coach and Author of *Understanding the Three Principles. Feel better; et more inner peace; Enjoy your life*

"What a wonderful book this is to read. The Three Principles explained in beautiful simplicity. Stories of hope and transformation, pointing to our innate health and wellbeing. The inside-out understanding, taught to me by some of the teachers in this book, transformed my life of misery – trapped in alcohol addiction – to a wonderful life of peace and wellbeing free from addiction.

The renowned Sydney Banks saved my life and I will be eternally grateful.

Thank you Sheela for writing this book and hopefully sparking transformation in the lives of the readers and their clients."

Sally Wyse, Addictions Coach and Counsellor

"If you are a coach or therapist and interested in how to draw out the wisdom, wellbeing and inspiration of your clients, this book is full of insightful and powerful orientations for your work. Reading through each chapter gives you an opportunity to experience the depth of each teacher, while also pointing you in the direction of greater impact and fulfilment in your work with others."

Barb Patterson, Conversations that Transform Your Business, Your Leadership, Your Life

"When I came across the Three Principles my life experience transformed dramatically – effortlessly and quickly.

As a doctor and a sexual and relationship therapist, I finally had the answers I'd been searching for over 30 years.

What became clear to me, as I'm sure you'll experience reading this book, is that all human suffering is based on simple misunderstandings around who and what we truly are and how the human experience is created. I also came to realise there is nothing wrong with any of us and nothing to fix in anyone.

If I had come across the Three Principles in my training as a doctor and psychotherapist it would have made such a huge difference to my practice and to my life."

Anne Curtis, former GP and Psychosexual Therapist

Inside Out Transformation

A Revolutionary Guide for Coaches, Therapists and Counsellors

Conversations with 15 Renowned Leaders

Sheela Masand

Cover design by: Nigel Smith www.nigelsmithart.com

Website: www.insideouttransformation.org

ISBN 978-84-09-41073-6

from my heart to yours

Table Of Contents

Foreword

In 1909, Sigmund Freud and Carl Jung headlined what the American Psychological Association has called "the most famous conference in the history of American psychology" at Clark University in Worcester, Massachusetts. Having grown up a stone's throw from Clark, I used to imagine what it would have been like to be in the room while the people at the forefront of a radically new model of human psychology compared notes about what they'd seen so far about making a difference with their fellow humans.

Imagine yourself as a budding student at that conference – someone with a sincere desire to have a positive impact in the lives of others. You're invited backstage to sit down with each one of these pioneers in their field and ask them questions – questions about the principles behind their work, their own personal philosophy, and their process.

What would you most want to know?

In the early 1970's, an equally radical new paradigm of human psychology came into being on Salt Spring Island in Canada. Based on the work of a Scottish welder, Sydney Banks, who had an enlightenment experience that transformed his way of seeing the world, this new understanding was often spoken about as the "inside-out understanding" and laid out in terms of three psycho-spiritual principles – divine Mind, divine Thought, and divine Consciousness.

First a few, then dozens, and now thousands of helping professionals have been drawn to Syd's insights, and together they have formulated a field that has spawned hundreds of books, and helped tens of thousands of people, to live happier, mentally healthier lives no matter how much they had been struggling and even suffering before coming across it.

I am one of those tens of thousands – not a psychologist but a student, teacher, and coach, seeking insight not only into what actually changed my own life for the better but also what consistently works to help other people's lives transform.

While I have been fortunate enough to get to know and even work with many of the people you will be reading about in this book, I was thrilled to "meet" each one of them again through the eyes of Sheela Masand, the intrepid interviewer who actually took her "backstage pass" and asked the questions that every serious student of transformation wants to know the answers to.

Questions like:

- How do you describe the work you do with others?
- What are the Three Principles?
- How do you prepare for a session?
- What's your intention with a client?

and perhaps my favourite:

- If there was one thing you could tell your younger self about working with clients, what would it be?

As you might expect, everyone answers each question differently. Some seem to take a quite psychological approach; some more practical; others a blatantly spiritual one. Some consider themselves therapists, coaches, or counsellors; others present as mentors, teachers, or guides.

Yet for all their differences in philosophy and approach, there are three things that you will notice in every one of the interviews that follows:

1. A deep respect for the quiet feeling of presence, love, and care and its essential impact in working with others.
2. A sense of awe at the power of thought to create our personal realities and at times, blind us to the innate health, creativity, resilience, and wisdom within.
3. A willingness to get in over their heads, not know what's going to happen, and let the intelligence of life beyond the intellect guide them in real time with their clients.

Here is my only advice as you set out on your own learning adventure:

As best you can, read this book with no agenda and nothing on your mind.

While you are no doubt here because you want to have more of an impact in your work, there is more on offer than you will find in the transcripts of each interview. If you are willing to take your time and give your mind the chance to settle as you go, you will find yourself "reading between the lines". The quiet feeling described throughout the book will bubble up inside you, and you will begin to get insights for yourself into the differences that make a difference with your clients.

The understanding behind the practices of these pioneering professionals transformed my life. My fondest wish is that they do the same for you and anyone fortunate enough to get the chance to sit down with you in the future to learn more about themselves and how life really works.

With all my love,
Michael Neill
Bestselling author of *The Inside-Out Revolution, Supercoach, and The Space Within*

Introduction

This book is one of the many ripples caused by the realisation of an ordinary man who had an extraordinary experience and chose to use a metaphor – The Three Principles of Universal Mind, Consciousness and Thought – as a pointer to what he discovered. His name was Sydney Banks. His simple, yet profound realisation transformed his own life immediately, and as he shared what he had seen it subsequently changed thousands upon thousands of lives and continues to do so to this day.

What did Syd see that was so transformational?

That's the million dollar question, of course! The answers will be revealed in various forms throughout this book via the voices of fifteen of Syd's early students. They were fortunate enough to know Syd and learn directly from him, enabling them to go on and share what they had seen with hundreds of thousands of clients over the years.

But you don't have to wait to read all the chapters for my answer to that question.

Simply put, it's *the truth of who-we-are and how it is veiled.*

Syd uncovered a description of how we function as human beings – from the inside-out.

Who-we-are is also often referred to as our true nature, love, peace, happiness, wisdom, wellbeing, innate health, home and many more words that try to describe the indescribable. Syd used the words “formless” and “impersonal" to point too.

The veil, as I call it, is often talked about as thoughts, thinking, beliefs, feelings, concepts, perceptions, emotions, psychology, etc. Syd also used the words “form” and “personal".

You may be wondering how seeing and understanding this would help clients experience transformation.

Imagine a client who wants to achieve a specific goal, but believes they are stuck with a particular personality trait that is holding them back. When they *insightfully* realise that the personality trait is an illusory concept (the veil) and their default is wellbeing (who-they-are), their shoulders drop, they breathe easier and their eyes light up. They understand they don’t need to keep searching for the magic bullet that will free them of the personality trait – the veil has been recognised for what it is. They are not broken and don’t need fixing. Suddenly a whole new world of possibility and potential has opened up for them and nothing on the outside has changed.

That’s transformation from the inside-out.

Notice I used the word *insightfully*. It’s a really important point. Something that Syd realised, that very few enlightened teachers talk about, is that the capacity for insight is “built into” every single human being. Insight doesn’t come to us through information gathering or using the intellect and trying to work something out. It’s a sight from within as Syd often described it, not something you find in the outside world. It’s literally a fresh new thought. A light bulb moment as many people describe it. Sometimes it's an inkling of something you know is shifting and can be difficult to put into words too.

It can happen at any moment because that's its nature which is really good news for humanity – time literally has no bearing on transformation. Syd's own experience is a powerful example of this fact. His life was literally transformed in moments. So much so, he turned to his wife and said,

"*I'm home. I'm free. I've made it. I've conquered this world. This means to say that you and I will be travelling all over the world. We're going to change psychology and psychiatry so millions of people will be healed.*"

At the time Syd was a welder living in Canada, living what would be described as a pretty normal everyday life. As you can imagine, his wife was totally taken aback! But it turned out to be true. He spent the next 36 years travelling the globe and sharing the Principles he had so miraculously uncovered.

These simple Principles (and throughout the book I will use a capital when referring to The Three Principles) are something largely invisible to the majority of people and yet the implications of understanding them are infinite.

To clarify how important principles are, take gravity, as an example. Its discovery explains so much of what we take for granted now – I drop a pen and it always falls to the floor, no exception. The implications of understanding the invisible principle of gravity are huge! One obvious demonstration is the fact that we are able to fly all over the world in metal objects! The principles of flight include an understanding of gravity, together with the principles of thrust, drag and lift. Getting a glimpse of the underlying principles of something can be life-changing.

Principles are by their very nature descriptive, constant and predictive. When we understand there are universal Principles to describe how we function as human beings, it means there is a system we can depend on 100% of the time. It does not discriminate between gender, nationality, colour or creed.

Working with clients from the inside-out always takes these universal Principles into consideration. We are working from the unshakable foundation of knowing that experience is created from the inside-out 100% of the time. No exceptions.

When we take into account the endless implications of Principles creating our human experience from the inside-out it's a true game-changer.

No longer do we have to attain goals to feel good, or find the solution to a problem to relieve stress, or make more money to feel secure. We are living in the feeling of our thinking, and not the feeling of the outside circumstances. Money can never make us feel secure, achieving goals can never make us feel good and stress can never be relieved by problem solving. That is huge and really good news.

We do not have to "do" or "not do" something to gain a certain feeling. Feelings come and go. It relieves the pressure of having to do or be anything. This is transformational. When someone insightfully sees that their feeling state is not dependent on the outside world they tend to say something along the lines of, "Nothing changed, but everything is different!" They have insight into a new reality that a few seconds ago did not exist. Nothing in the outside world changed, but their experience of it did. That's transformation.

Who doesn't want to get off the hamster wheel of constant problem solving? Who doesn't want to live a life knowing that their experiences are never anything to be afraid of? Who doesn't want to know that to feel the joy, peace and love, that is our true nature, we don't have to do anything or go anywhere?

Sydney Banks realised that we are so much more than the thoughts and feelings we experience. He pointed to it over and over again in as many ways as he could, as innumerous sages and spiritual teachers also have throughout the ages. The beauty of being able to use Principles to point to something that is formless and totally mystical, makes it a little easier to grasp.

Understanding the spiritual nature of who/what we are and how we function psychologically has transformed the lives of countless individuals in many different walks of life. The possibility of discovering wellbeing as our default setting is available to every single human being at any time and anywhere. It has taken addicts off the street, reduced the murder rate to zero in a low income housing project, enabled ex-prisoners to help others like themselves because they have felt more freedom in jail than they have ever experienced in their life before! And the everyday concerns of parenting, finances, relationships, business, physical health, mental health and so much more can be added to the list.

The coaches, therapists and mentors in this book have all witnessed these types of results with clients, some of which you will hear about. What you won't hear about is the "right" way to do this work with clients. This was my main observation throughout the interviews – there is no "right" way.

Please know that this is not meant to be an instructional handbook on "how to", but a collection of experiences, insights, thoughts and ideas of those who learned directly from Sydney Banks. A valuable resource of the "first generation" or "elders" as they are often referred to. You will hear, see and feel what's right for you in the moment and that will be different for each person because that's the nature of being human.

In the spirit of staying as close to their voices as possible, I didn't heavily edit because I wanted to hear their personality come through. If you know them personally, or have heard them speak, you will recognise their voice. The ideas generously shared are theirs, not mine, and the quotes shared at the beginning of each chapter were chosen by them.

To get the most out of the chapters, I suggest you read with an open mind, wondering what insights might occur to you rather than agreeing or disagreeing, or looking for a fit to any other model of therapy or coaching. It's easy to do the latter and it won't be of the greatest service to you. Believe me, I know! I've done my fair share of comparing and discounting along the way. But when we listen without filters, listen for insight, listen as if we know nothing, there is far more chance of something being realised and/or felt that is meaningful and transformational. This is a fundamental piece of all transformation – a willingness to listen without "what we think we already know" getting in the way.

You'll also find some of this advice described in the chapters. The importance of deep listening is addressed by every single one of the coaches, therapists and mentors in this book. You will find an extensive explanation by Jack Pranksy in his chapter. It is fundamental to assisting with any type of transformation for human beings because when we are in the business of highlighting the infinite potential of human beings, we have to be in the business of deep listening.

Please enjoy your journey with each wonderful contributor. If you would like to explore more of their work, you will find details at the end of the book under Resources.

Chapter One

Jack Pransky PhD

"All we are is peace, love and wisdom and the power to create the illusion that we're not."
Jack Pransky

What are The Three Principles?

After studying this inside-out direction for about twenty-seven years it suddenly came to me in a flash out of the blue in one simple statement what the Three Principles are all about. It's the statement you have at the top of this chapter: "All we are is peace, love and wisdom, and the power to create the illusion that we're not." Simplicity!

To me, this means the Principles are really about only two things:

1. Built into everyone's spiritual essence is pure peace of mind, pure love, and pure wisdom that comes through us as new insight. It brings us automatic wellbeing and innate mental health that we couldn't get away from even if we wanted to. It arises within us from the pure Intelligence of Universal Mind

coming into our pure Consciousness, and we experience it when our mind clears or quietens.

2. We can only create the illusion that we are not this pure essence by (usually inadvertently) using our incredible power of Thought against ourselves. Whatever we think, we experience, because, as I said, the power of Consciousness picks up whatever thoughts we have and gives us a "real" experience of them; in other words, we believe we're seeing and feeling "reality" when, really, it is only our own creative power of thought making it look and feel that way. So, instead of experiencing the pure essence of who we really are, we often experience ego and/or fear and all that arises from these.

Luckily, we can be aware of how it all really works within us from the inside-out. It is extremely humbling to realise we already are our pure spiritual essence, and the only reason we're not having an experience of it is because we're believing the thinking that tells us we're not. Also extremely humbling is to realise, as I said before, that the outside world – what people say and do to us and the situations and circumstances in which we find ourselves – can *never* make us feel anything; it is *always and only* our own thinking about those things that makes us feel everything we do.

That's how I see it anyway, for what it's worth. Simplicity itself – something Syd Banks was always hoping we would see, and we kept making it way too complicated.

How do you describe what you do?

What I do is point people to how their experience of life is created–the way it really works inside them–and I point to how deep within their spiritual essence, they are already everything they are looking for in life and it has only been inadvertently "covered up" by their own thinking.

But I have to begin where they're at. They're going to come in with their presenting "problems", and the means to the end is "deep listening". By deeply listening to them I hope to help guide them ultimately to realise from within the way their experience of life works, moment to moment through the interplay of Universal Mind, Consciousness and Thought.

I've come to see that there are *only* three things going on, always.

1. There is whatever is happening in the outside world.
2. There is the meaning we make of it for ourselves with our own thinking.
3. And underneath all that, there is the essence of who we are connected to the Oneness of all things.

That's all that's ever going on! I have found recently that it's so helpful for people to make the distinction between the truth of what is actually happening out there – the actual behaviours of people and/or the words and tone they are using – and everything else. And what "everything else" means is the way they use their thinking to make meaning for themselves.

For example, if a loved one dies and her partner is in a state of total sorrow so much she can't even function, all that has happened, really, is her loved one has died and is no longer with her. That's in the outside world. That's the truth. Then she takes her incredible gift of the power of Thought and thoughts come to her about the fact that he is no longer there and what that means for her and her life. For example; thoughts of sadness, or thoughts of sorrow, or thoughts of despair, or thoughts of worry about her own life now, or thoughts of anger that she is left behind, or thoughts of gratefulness that she had the time she had with him, whatever. All of those are inadvertently made up. There is no one right way to see it. They are all fine; it's just that we have to live with whichever one we inadvertently come up with.

It makes perfect sense for someone who has lost a loved one to feel sadness – even possibly sorrow, but for how long? If she is still feeling so much sorrow that she can't function five years later, I'm not sure most of us would think that healthy. Then, Consciousness instantly picks up that thought of sorrow, or whatever she happens to think at the time, and sends it through her senses and, from that, she gets a "real" feeling of it and it sure looks and feels like a "real" experience. She believes her sorrow is coming from the fact that he died. But if her partner were emotionally abusing her, for example, she may have a different thought-feeling-experience than sorrow; she might feel relief.

One of the things that helps people recover is when they see their feeling is not coming from what happened to them out there, but instead is coming from their own thinking about what happened, and they could think a myriad of different things, some at a higher or lower level of consciousness than what they're experiencing now. When any of us sees this, our experience then shifts, because we know we're not stuck with whatever we're feeling now. Even if we can't get ourselves out of the sorrow right now, when we truly know we're 100% responsible for the experience we're getting and that experience will shift when our thinking shifts and thoughts are always changing, it becomes a lot more difficult to stay stuck.

If the outside world was doing it to us we'd be stuck with the feeling until the outside world changes, but when people see that their experience changes when their thinking changes, it gives them back their power; they can see they've been giving up their power to the outside world. I'm not saying people have control over most of what they think, because they don't; I am saying they can realise they're not at the mercy of the outside world. Very often people think they are.

Another example: If somebody has a physical problem, such as a hip that needs replacing or cancer, that physical issue is a fact. Then there's the meaning that person makes of it for himself. The meaning that person ascribes to that fact becomes his experience of it. It's not that the physical problem will be different – the physical issue is what it is (I won't even get into the power of thought some people have mustered to beat cancer that doctors proclaimed hopeless) – but the relationship we have to it with our own thinking is what gives us our experience of it.

What's the driver behind the way you work? Your philosophy?

If I have any philosophy in working with clients it's that everyone has within them perfect mental health. It's part of our soul, built into us. It's pure consciousness – consciousness uncontaminated by any thoughts – connected to the Oneness of All things. It's within everyone. As I said, the reason people walk around looking like they don't have perfect mental health is because they think thoughts that appear to inadvertently cover this health up. So in my work with clients I see this essence in everyone with whom I come into contact – even if they can't see it in themselves. And I know that at any moment, no matter how bad things look, people are capable of touching that place, because it is who they really are. And that place of pure Health and wisdom is what cures. I hope to be able to point people there.

If there was one thing you could tell your younger self about working with clients, what would it be?

I'm going to give you a roundabout answer. I came into this work through prevention. Prevention was my field. I never intended to be a counsellor. In fact, I couldn't stand the idea of what a counsellor usually does: sitting down with people all day talking about their problems. That idea did not appeal to me at all. But *preventing* problems, such as alcohol and drug abuse, delinquency, child abuse and neglect and all that stuff – preventing these things *before* they become problems, was always very, very intriguing and hopeful to me. This includes prevention of mental disorders or distress.

It was only when I found the Principles and started doing trainings in prevention from the inside-out that it eventually led me into coaching, because after my trainings people would ask me if they could talk to me individually. I then realised I enjoyed talking with people one on one and, to my amazement, I found myself actually being helpful to them. So that's how it evolved for me. I had no coaching or counselling experience whatsoever. I just kind of made it up as I went along.

At the beginning the biggest problem I had, which is the biggest problem I see most people have when they learn the Principles, is that I wanted to beat people over the head with how incredible this stuff is, because it worked wonders both for me and for the people in low-income communities that I interviewed for *Modello*, which I wrote because of prevention. What we saw for ourselves was so beautiful and so uplifting that in our enthusiasm to spread it to the world we sometimes got a little overzealous or overbearing, which turned off some people. That happened to me at the beginning, and I still see that it happens a fair amount with others at the beginning.

I think in the old days I had something on my mind: "I want people to see these Principles in action for themselves because I know it will be helpful to them". As soon as I have a thought like that on my mind, all listening goes out of the window. So I have to take that completely off my mind and listen pure, untainted by my ideas, untainted by anything about *me*. So if I listen purely with nothing on my mind I'm going to hear what I need to hear to help them go where they need to go. So, the biggest suggestion I have for my younger self or for anyone getting into this initially is to consider any and all ideas in this regard completely irrelevant, which keeps our minds from holding onto them. Why would we hold onto something completely irrelevant?

The other thing I would say – this one didn't happen so much for me, but since I have often taught people how to be Principles-based coaches and trainers, I've seen it happen with many others – is that people start getting this thing about money. Like, "Uh-oh, people are paying me now, so I'd better deliver". That automatically points in the wrong direction because it's pointing to "me"; it's pointing to "I". If we have "I" or "me" in the picture when attempting to help others, it throws us completely off track. If we are going to be helpful to others it's important to let go of any ideas about the way we should be or even that we need to accomplish anything. That sounds like a paradox. But if we want to help people we have to forget about helping them; that's the paradox.

Also a paradox is the fact that somebody wants to work with clients or teach The Three Principles because of an insight on their part and wants to specifically share the Principles, and then not having that on top of one's mind? What's the point?

The point is simply to be of service to people. I want to be of service in any way they want me to be of service. When the way they want me to be of service meshes with the understanding of the Three Principles, that's when it works out best. But I don't want to thrust the Principles upon them; that's not my job. My job is to be of service to them. Now, if through my deep listening I think understanding the Three Principles will be the most helpful thing for them to grasp for me to be of service, and that often happens, great! But I might do a session with somebody and not even mention the Principles at all because in that moment I see being of service to them, which takes me in a different direction, is more important, which comes out of deep listening.

Afterwards, I might suggest to them that there may be something more to see about this; are they interested? It's helpful to get permission from a client. We want them to be all ears. If they are not ready to hear, we might as well save our breath. If we are going to talk about the Principles they have to be ready to hear it or they're not going to hear it. I'm not saying "permission" is a technique, but saying something like, "Would you like to hear how your experience is being created here?" Or, "Might you be interested in seeing how this really works within you?" Sometimes people will just give lip service to it, but our listening will tell us if they are saying yes but it's not really a yes. So we have to listen deeper. There's some block there that we want to listen to deeper. We might ask questions or throw out stuff to see if anything takes hold.

Do you prepare for a client session and if so, how?

Because we don't know what's going to happen in any client session, I think the worst thing we can do is try and predict where someone is going to go or if we want them to get somewhere. The only preparation is a good feeling and an empty mind. I never thought of it like that before; I like that. That's my preparation. Anything else gets in the way. Most times these days I say a little prayer beforehand, which brings me right into the moment and grounds me. But that's just me. The feeling plus listening is everything to me.

What's your intention with a client, if any? Are you trying to get them to see anything?

This gets back to my statement about being in service to them. I'm not taking them to what I want them to see – *at all. "At all"* is a very important statement. If I get an insight, through my listening, that taking them to a particular place would be helpful to this person, even if it sounds really weird, then I'm going to go there. But that comes out of the moment; it doesn't come out of an agenda. I've said this before, but the worst thing I could have on my mind is I've got to teach them the Three Principles.

Is there a process to your client work? Does the process have any components?

I see that there are four components or stages – I don't know what to call them. The first stage happens the moment before I walk into the room, before I even sit down with the person. I have to be the model of health, at least during the coaching experience. So I can't lose myself. For example, if somebody starts giving me a hard time, I can't get caught in that. I have to stay in my health.

What does "health" mean to you?

It's that state of pure mental health within our very soul, as I spoke of earlier. I have to be grounded in the understanding of the Three Principles, myself; meaning, I have to see myself and life through those eyes. I have to live from the spirit of the Three Principles. That has to come through during the coaching or counselling or therapy experience.

What does "living the spirit of the Three Principles" mean?

If life is levels of consciousness I have to recognise enough about what is happening within me so that I'm not pulled down by what happens in the outside world, because I'm seeing my experience of life coming from within me. So long as I'm seeing where my experience really comes from, in those moments I'm seeing it, I'm at a higher level of consciousness than people who believe their experience is coming from what is happening in the outside world. Or we could say living from one's health is living the spirit of the Principles.

I'm not saying we're in a la-di-dah state; we just need to know where our experience is coming from and what the true source of our health is. If we're really bummed out and down in the dumps, so long as we know our experience is coming from us, we are okay. If we think we're at the mercy of the outside world then we are going to get really low by uncomfortable things happening out there. But if I am low and see my experience is coming from me, it doesn't really matter if I'm low, so long as I know where it's coming from, because I know it's my own thinking and it will eventually shift so I'm not stuck with it, it's going to lift, and that's automatic hope!

Also automatic hope is what is embedded in the essence of who we are, embedded in pure consciousness beyond thought. As I said, it's pure peace of mind, pure love, pure wisdom. So when we see this for ourselves at any moment, we are connected to the real spirit of the Principles, and when we lose it – because in human form nobody can be there all the time, at least that I know of –when we drop, do we still realise that the experience is coming from us? Good enough for me.

So that's the first "step", so to speak: I am bringing my health to the table. Even if I am going through something I'm calling really hard in my own life, as soon as I walk in the door it all falls away and I am 100% present. If it doesn't, I'm useless.

Secondly, they are going to come in with a lot of stuff on their minds that is going to make their mind tight, you could say. Chances are, that's what they are doing or they wouldn't be coming to me. I want to do whatever I can to loosen up their mind, to help their mind relax its grip. The more lighthearted I am, the more friendly I am, the more we're sitting together as if talking on a front porch or by a fireplace, the more fun we have – whatever helps the mind to relax – that's what I want to achieve here. Anything that will help the mind calm down. But it has to be genuine because if it isn't they are going to see right through it and run in the other direction. Just the fact that we see the other person sitting in front of us as their health instead of their presenting problem, that will relax their mind a little because they will feel it from us – it feels nice to be in the presence of someone who cares for you. Whatever relaxes the mind, rapport, whatever it is, there is no sense saying anything if it's just going to bounce off a really tight mind.

The third "component" is "deep listening". To me it's the most critical part of anything we do in this work.

Would you say something more about how you see deep listening, since it's something you teach so much and have seen so much about?

I would say deep listening is dropping into a state of nothingness. We are completely blank. We are an empty vessel. We are taking the other person in purely (or as purely as possible). My partner says it's like listening to the rain. That's a good description. To really stay in a state of blankness, nothing-ness, empty-vessel-ness, "I don't know"-ness, is huge.

What gets in the way of that? It can only be one thing: our thoughts. We want no thoughts at all in our way. I have taught deep listening to probably thousands of people, and many do not realise at first that when they are listening to others they will have thoughts. Can't help that, but what do we do with those thoughts when they get there? If we hold onto them and start following them because, really, we think our own thoughts are more important than the client, we will lose the client. It's so innocent.

I have observed that, generally, four types of thoughts get in the way of deep listening most. I'm not saying these are the only thoughts that get in the way, but in my experience these are the most common: 1) distractions – we get distracted by something; 2) what I know – we think we know things; 3) "me" thoughts or ego thoughts – thinking it has something to do with me; 4) solutions – we try to solve their problem.

From my experience, these types of thoughts are what take people away from listening most. To counter this, we just have to have a sense of, or one eye on, or one ear on, seeing ourselves go off in those or other ways. We can set our intention beforehand to just *be* with the person in *love*, so to speak. When we go off of that into our minds and leave the other person – we have lost them; they are no longer in our consciousness. Our own thoughts are. But if I know those thoughts are irrelevant – completely unimportant – and can only get in the way, such thoughts tend to fall away on their own.

The other thing people commonly miss about deep listening is that the intelligence behind life has all the answers. An answer exists about what is behind this problem, and an answer exists about the solution. This answer is embedded in the spiritual, intelligent energy (Divine Mind) swirling all around us, within us and between us. If I'm truly deep listening I am listening to that spiritual Mind energy. The words of the other person can actually get in the way, so I don't really want to listen to their words. I want to listen way beyond their words, and there's really no way to describe it. That person might not have a clue what the answer is, yet s/he really knows the answer is deep, deep, deep inside him or herself because it's embedded in this pure energy-intelligence, embedded in pure consciousness. That's what we're ultimately listening for.

The paradox is we can't intentionally listen for it; we have to listen by being that empty vessel and not get distracted by extraneous thoughts, and sometimes the answer appears. It's like a pipeline to universal intelligence that tells us what the problem *really* is – not the presenting problem but what the person is not seeing and ultimately what the person really needs to hear to spawn insights themselves that lifts them up and brings them to a higher level of consciousness.

Sometimes I will be listening to a client and will find myself puzzled. People come up with things that don't make sense to me. For example, they say they want to have more money in their life, yet they have distressing thoughts about money and believe those distressing thoughts are aiding them somehow. That's puzzling! What does distressed thinking about money have to do with bringing in more money? I get puzzled about that. Distressed thinking actually works counter to it because we don't have a clear mind so we have less of a chance to hear wisdom speak about what we need to do to get or save more. So, if I am puzzled by it I want to help them be puzzled by it for themselves. Helping people be puzzled about themselves can be really, really helpful.

Another example is looking for a love relationship. You want to find a love relationship but you're distressed that you're not going to find one. It's puzzling that people would hold on to distressed thoughts, thinking it will better produce a love relationship, when it works against it. There are so many things to be puzzled about. But I am not *trying* to be puzzled; through my deep listening I get a hit that something doesn't compute.

Can I help that person take a look at that so s/he gets puzzled about it? All that comes out of deep listening.

People come in seeing some "reality" driving them, and I want to help them call that reality into question; like, is this really true? That kind of questioning leads to seeing the way the Three Principles work within us to give us our experience. So I'm pointing people there, but I'm not leading them – another paradox. I'm just going with where listening takes me, but I know, way in the back of my mind that if people really see where experience comes from, they'll do better. It's not really a goal. It's tricky. It's not an aspiration because as soon as you have that on your mind that it's a goal, suddenly listening goes out of the window.

Deep Listening is the only guide. It will take us to what people need to hear. At that point, what they need to hear becomes the goal, so to speak. When it coincides with what the understanding of the Principles is telling us, it's a beautiful thing. That's when I think it works the best. Now we've jumped to the fourth component of the process. *Only when I get a hit from wisdom*, which comes out of deep listening, do I resort to what one might call teaching or, more accurately, drawing out what people really know deep inside but don't know that they know. But this happens *only* when I have such an insight. Only then do I want to say anything I think might be important for them or about the Three Principles (and then only when I believe it will be relevant to them). Before then, I will ask questions that come to me in the moment and/or throw out things to see if they take hold, but that is all part of the deep listening process. I'm listening to their responses, which mostly prompts me to ask more and listen even deeper. Keep in mind, until I get hit with an insight I have no idea where I'm going. I'm in "I don't know" mode. But once I see something I know they need to hear, I'll help them be "all ears". Ideally, just by questioning and listening they will get hit with their own insights. I would much rather have that happen than go into teaching. If they're not getting there by my listening and questioning, sometimes I have to teach, but I don't want to do it too soon.

For them to have their own insights is the ultimate. Short of that, or along with that, I want them to be in a good feeling. So those two things: a good feeling and insights help them with their life. The reason a good feeling helps is because their mind calms down and they have a better chance, even after the session ends, of having insights that help them with their life. But as I always say, since there is no way to ever make an insight happen in anybody, what can we do? We can know that the more their mind relaxes and the more I'm able to listen deeply to them, the better chance there is to have insights.

So, in summary, the four components or stages, as I see them, are 1) Being in my own health and bringing that into the session; 2) helping people's minds calm down; 3) deep listening; 4) helping people see the Principles in action in relation to their issue. But that leads to the most important component that we have no control over: 5) them having their own insights and being able to generalise it to all issues and all people. I use the same "process" whether I'm coaching, counselling or doing therapy. I know some people won't agree with this but, to me, they are all the same; maybe only at different levels or intensity. I also use the same "process" if I'm teaching or doing trainings or helping a community or an organisation.

What happens within you if you get into trouble with a client? What do you do?

Don't forget, I said I spend most of my time in "I don't know" mode. Here's the way it looks: I don't know, I don't know, I don't know, I don't know, I may ask a question that occurs to me in the moment, I don't know, I may throw out a comment to see what happens, I don't know, I don't know, I don't know, oh, I know something! I just heard it. I don't want to talk out of anything except if I'm struck by something that seems really important.

So within that process, what does getting into trouble mean? Getting into trouble might mean they think I'm full of s**t, but why would they if we're just in a good feeling together and I'm listening to them? What I am talking about is preventing getting into trouble with a client. Being in "I don't know", good feeling, listening – it's tough to get into trouble doing that. I used to get into trouble with clients and not know where to go with them, but now I can't even remember the last time I had trouble with a client.

So, what could getting into trouble with a client mean? I'm not getting anywhere with them? Okay, there are a few clients I may not get anywhere with – although that's rare for me these days. You know what that means to me? It means I'm not listening deeply enough. If that happens I want to go back to the drawing board, go back to deep listening. In that case, I want to go into deep, deep, deep listening!

We only scratch the surface with our listening. Psychics listen at such a deep level that they pick up things we don't. Well, we could all listen at that level. There is no limit to the depth of our listening and if I'm not getting anywhere with a client, if that's how getting into trouble is defined, then I just want to go back to deep, deep, deep listening.

What other ways do you think we could get into trouble with clients? What have you run into that you would call trouble?

A feeling of people haven't got what they came for?

This is where being of service comes in, if I am totally in service, how could they not get what they came for?

Maybe they have an idea of what they want by the end of the session and it hasn't happened for them?

Okay. I would ask them more about what they want and what's behind it, and go into listening about that. That would be puzzling to me. We're coming to the end of the session and they are saying they aren't getting what they came for. "Okay, tell me again, what did you come for?" It's like really getting down to how can I be of more help to that person? How can I be of more service? Stuff like that keeps us out of trouble and it's sincere; we sincerely want to be of service or help to them.

What about someone who does not have insights over a period of time and there appears to be no sign of shifts?

Sometimes people are so caught by their own thinking, it's like they are in jail, or they have this band around their head or something like a vice grip on their head. Sometimes we may not be able to penetrate it, but I still think the answer is deeper listening, I still do. I think we have not been able yet to listen deeply enough in that situation. What is the wall that's blocking them? A fascinating thing to listen for.

Is problem solving for a client the end of the story or do you go further?

Way further. Problem solving is not the issue. Problem solving is not even the solution. So we solved one problem, but if they don't understand how things work some other problem is going to surface that they find is just as much of a problem. We want to help them see beyond the problem to the way things work. That's what will help them. Whatever problem comes up, our experience only works one way. That's what I meant before when I said generalising it. How can we help them see it's not only this problem; it's any problem that comes up? And not only any problem that comes up for the client; any problem that comes up for anyone. It's always the same stuff going on. Not only that, do they see that their "problem" – any problem – is really only an illusion of their own creation? When they can see that, we know we've gone deep. This is where Three Principles coaching/counselling/psychotherapy departs from other approaches.

Actually, in my view, there are two major ways of where it departs from other approaches: 1) all our problems are illusions – of course, you can't just say that to people because you might get punched in the face or something, but you can listen to people deeply enough where they will eventually come to see that for themselves. 2) The other thing is *Knowing* that we are all whole, healthy, safe, that our essence cannot be touched by whatever alleged "problems" we have.

So, if people come in seeing "reality" and instead we help them see "illusion of my own creation", imagine how huge that is! If people come in believing they're broken and we help them see how they are really fine and perfectly whole, imagine how huge that is! That's what will lift them, realising those two things, and then they'll be in great shape to deal with any "problems" that come up – until they forget or where they have blind spots, and then they won't see it, like I don't in some areas. I would say every Three Principles coach or teacher has his or her own blind spots. We all do! We're human. There are some things we still see as "reality" and sometimes we are going to forget. Yet, with our understanding we have this backdrop in the back of our mind of the way we function. We may forget in a moment but we are eventually going to see it again. Ideally that's what we hope our clients will see.

We can be of service to our clients in the hope they see that. If they don't – and this is what I also would suggest to people starting out – it's not our responsibility! We can't take the responsibility for whether somebody else has an insight or not. All we can do is our best. That's what we want to take responsibility for: doing our best – the best we can see at the time.

Is this a paradox? You say you sometimes don't share the Principles in a session with a client and there is no intention apart from being of service, and then you say you want to share the Three Principles.

That's something to be puzzled about, right? The point is, I'm not forcing the Principles on anybody, ever. Even if I think it would be helpful to them, if they don't want to go there, it would be silly for me to go there because they're not going to hear me anyway. I am being of service to them in the way they want, then once I'm in service to them and they don't want to go anywhere near the Principles, it might occur to me to ask them a question that might take them further in that direction. But that will either occur to me or it won't. If it doesn't occur to me, fine. But that's just me.

I'm still coming to terms with being with clients without sharing the Three Principles if that's the way it goes.

Well, do you feel obligated?

Obligated is a strong term.

That's why I asked it like that.

It's a bit like it's a disservice if I'm not sharing them, but as you say, through deep listening we know whether people are open to hearing or not.

What would be the sense of sharing it if people are not going to be able to hear it? We are just wasting our breath, just talking about our own ideas at that point. I want to be of service first, then that might occur to me. Being of service to me is enough. If I never get there it's only because they are not open to hearing it. That's okay; it's not my job to get people to see the understanding, it's my job to be of service. I would say 19 times out of 20, in my experience, they become open to hearing it. That's great.

Is the feeling important for you when coaching?

Yes, the feeling and understanding are everything.

Could you share a story or stories on what worked well and what didn't and what are the takeaways for you?

I'm not meaning this to be a plug for my books – or maybe I am – but in both *Somebody Should Have Told Us!* (in Chapter XI) and *Seduced by Consciousness* (in Chapter 40) I have two actual recorded transcripts, respectively, of coaching sessions that appeared to work out very well, as well as numerous other descriptions of working with clients, so I would just point people to those.

Thank you for allowing me to be part of this book

Chapter Two

Sandra Krot

"With our intellect we discover. With an insight, we uncover."
Sydney Banks

How do you describe the work you do with clients?

I always like to say that I am in the business of putting myself out of business. My work is informed by what has become known as the Three Principles. These Principles explain that all human experience, including the experience of our problems, is being created inside our minds AND that all answers we are looking for are inside as well. Therefore, when I work with clients my primary focus is to help them to unlock their own insights. Everything I do is in service of this goal.

What are The Three Principles?

The Three Principles make up our essential nature and they create our psychological functioning. They are invisible forces that allow us to be resilient, to have insights and to change. Because the Principles are invisible, we tend not to talk about them but they are critical to our understanding of the human condition. The Principle of Mind refers to the intelligent energy that makes life possible. This intelligence grows the plants, beats our heart, knows all things. The Principle of Consciousness allows us to be aware of our experience in the moment as well as to be aware of the intelligence behind life. The Principle of Thought gives us the power to think and to create. How we use these Three Principles determines our moment to moment experience. Realising these Principles helps us get upstream of our feelings and behaviour.

What's the driver behind the way you work with clients? Your philosophy?

There are two. The first one is I am trying to help my clients find answers for themselves, that's what drives me. What do they need help with? What question does my client have? What would be meaningful for them? That's job number one for me, to find that out.

The second thing is to teach them how their mind works. Whatever their question, their problem, their challenge, I know that if they understand how their mind works they are going to find the answers that they seek, but I've got to know what they are looking for first. In my mind, that's one of the mistakes that Three Principles practitioners make. They are very excited and enthusiastic about sharing an understanding of the Three Principles, and they often skip the step of finding out what the client really needs. They forget to listen to the client deeply. Without this step, the Principles can sound generic. A generic understanding can be helpful but not impactful. My philosophy is to find out what question the client has, what they are looking to answer, what can I help them answer.

If there was one thing you could tell your younger self about working with clients, what would it be?

Listening. Honestly, I can't believe how often I skipped this step in my early career, innocently. I was so excited to share. I did this with my family and friends. I used to invite someone out for coffee and I would spill all over them and after a while it would be "don't have coffee with Sandy!" I was so excited and I was puzzled as to why people weren't as excited as me. It took a long time to realise how critical listening was. I needed to learn how my client saw the world. What did they already know to be true? Where were they already using their minds well? I wanted to have some sort of reference point I could point to. Listening was a big lesson for me. I read a quote and it's been in the back of my mind for decades – something like this, "learning is mostly talking and teaching is mostly listening" – and that's how I work, that's my philosophy.

Do you prepare for a client session and if so, how?

I almost always do. It may not be right before a session. It might begin at the end of the last session. I hold the client in my mind very gently and I go about my day. Periodically they will cross my mind and sometimes what happens is a phrase that they said comes to mind that I heard when we were in session, but I didn't address it at the time or I didn't see any significance to it. I will tuck that phrase away and I'll ask about it later. I'll wonder why they used that phrase. So I do a lot of reflecting on my clients in the gap between one session and the next session and it really helps me. It's not that I show up to the next session loaded with questions, but all my reflection seems to inform me once the new session begins.

What's your intention with a client, if any? Are you trying to get them to see anything?

I want them to solve their own problems. And not just the particular problem they come to me with. That's the beauty of learning the Principles. It's the beauty of learning how your mind works because you take your mind wherever you go. I do a lot of coaching with businesses and we work with many different groups within a business; I can show up in a business and see a person I coached maybe six months or a year earlier. I love it when they let me know they appreciated what they learned and it wasn't just for their problem, it wasn't just for their time management issue, it helped them with their teenagers too!

I want them to solve whatever challenge they think is bringing them to a session and again I want it to be their definition of the problem, not my definition. Sometimes I get people referred to me by their leaders so they are "volun-told" to come to see me. Their leader may have the desire that they learn a particular thing, and whilst it's in my equation, that's not going to be my focal point. I really want to find out what the client wants to learn. The very first session with me, I call a goal setting session where I will ask questions like, "Where do you want to go?" or "If a miracle happened and you could change, what would you change?" or "If you had a magic wand and something could change about you, not about your job or your circumstances, but about you, what would it be?" We make a list and it's their list and that's what we are shooting for.

Is there a process to your client work? Components?

The very first thing before taking on a client, I insist on making sure they are on board. I get people referred to me by their bosses. In fact I just worked with someone this past week who was referred to me by his boss. I wouldn't take him on until I had had a number of phone calls making sure he was on board.

I pressed him, "Why do you want to come for coaching?"

"Well Linda told me I had to do it."

"No, that's not good enough!"

"Really, why?"

With him I had to have a few phone calls and I don't charge for these calls. These are really to see if he is on board with working together and if I am the right fit. That's step one and it takes however long it takes.

Step two is goal setting. What do you want to learn? What do you want to change? What do you think needs to change? What do you think the problem is? We come up with a set of goals even though it's kind of ironic that I spend time doing this because the thing about learning the Principles is that people are going to have insights. And one of the things they are going to have insights about is what the actual problem is. I realise it's not a perfect system, but it's a place to start. Then we revisit these goals, and this is when the beauty happens, they look back and say, "Wow, that wasn't it, was it? No, that wasn't it, now I see something completely different". That's a process that happens throughout the session.

Once I feel I understand what the client wants, what the goals are, what problems they think they need to solve and once I feel I have a good grasp of that, then I begin the process of sharing with them how their mind works.

There are two points I want to make. The first is that the human mind has a built-in design for success, this is in our book (*Invisible Power*). I want them to know that built into their make-up, built into their mind, is the capacity to find the answers they are looking for. They are not missing anything, there is nothing wrong with them that an insight can't solve. I want them to know the capacity for insight is built into them and it can happen at any time under any circumstances, no matter how big the problem is, no matter how long they have had the problem, no matter how many people have told them they are hopeless, it doesn't matter. Your mind is designed to serve you well, there is nothing wrong with the design of the system. I try to get that point across in spades.

The second point I want to make is that your mind works only one way – it works from the inside-out. I want to share with them that there is a paradigm that determines how experience gets created in humanity and there is only one paradigm, there's not two, there's not five, there is one. It's inside-out and I want them to insightfully see that because that's what's going to bail them out. That's what's going to wake them up in the moment when their habit is in full force and directing their behaviour – I want them to remember where their experience is coming from. In the heat of the moment, when they are upset, I want them to remember where their feelings are coming from. That realisation settles them down and once that "settled-downess" happens, all kinds of things are possible, all kinds of new thoughts, new visions, new listening and questions will show up in their minds and will guide them.

So those are the two points I spend the rest of my time on with my client until we mutually feel they have had the insights they need to now go out and live without my coaching and then we say goodbye.

From what you have been explaining it sounds like you don't do single sessions – do you have packages or programmes?

Yes, my clients come to me through my corporate work. When I take on a client I want to make sure I have a consistent amount of time without a lot of interruption. There are two ways to work with me. Either they have taken a corporate programme with Insight Principles, i.e., taken a group programme with their teams, or they have come to me directly. When clients come to me directly, I ask them to spend four days in an intensive, followed by nine months coaching via phone or video conferencing. If somebody I personally know and have had a lot of contact with asks for a couple of sessions, I'll do that. I rarely do single sessions because I think it takes a bit of time to really impact people. First it takes time to get to know people and find out what they really want, then to get an understanding of these Principles across to people and for them to have time to have their own insights. They need to see what occurs to them when they are in their day-to-day life. I like to design multi-session packages.

What happens within you if you get into trouble with a client? What do you do?

Working with clients is unpredictable. I've had clients realise something profound that changes everything, in our first 15 minutes together. Others have a more incremental path of mini insights and gradual improvement. Also from time to time my client and I seem to get stuck or even take steps backwards.

What happens inside me when there is an apparent road block is, of course, determined by the thinking I'm entertaining in that moment. Sometimes, I find myself impatient and bothered (at the client or at myself) for the lack of movement. My thinking is typically filled with judgment. When I wake up to what is going on inside, my mind can self-correct and I can return to being helpful to the client. If I don't wake up, not much progress gets made.

Fortunately, most of the time when I notice the lack of movement or insight, I get curious. I wonder what I missed. I wonder what the client is hearing/has heard. I start over. I might ask the client to tell me what they hope will happen as a result of us working together. Why did they come to see me in the first place? I might ask what they have learned so far. I keep asking questions and I usually hear something new which sparks new dialogue.

Our minds are designed to have insight. We've been having insights since the day we were born. I know (and I want the client to know) that an insight can show up at any time that will guide us toward the next step. Part of my job as a practitioner is to remind clients about this fact.

Is problem solving for a client the end of the story? Or do you go further?

Most of the time the clients I work with are superior problem solvers, I mean superior problem solvers, that's the problem! They have come at their particular issue the way they always come at things, very analytically, very memory driven, very push, push – putting their weight into it – that's the corporate world. It's the state-of-the-art in the corporate world as far as I can see and it works for certain kinds of problems.

However, so many problems that companies and individuals face today are very complex and a number of them are human related. This kind of pushing and driving and problem solving doesn't work.

I'm introducing them to a whole new muscle, if you will. That's often what we say: sometimes when you go to physiotherapy they isolate a muscle, it tends to be a weak muscle and what you discover is other muscles compensate for it and so this weak muscle never gets used. When the physiotherapist isolates it, it hurts because you haven't used it or maybe it was injured. We are isolating an insight muscle you haven't used and it's not comfortable at first, but we want people to trust us that this is a different way of solving their problem, to solve a problem through insight. It's allowing their mind to work the way it's designed to work, to bring them something new, to bring them a new thought as opposed to muscling it, working it out or figuring it out.

Again, not that it's bad to work on things. I never want to give clients the impression that problem solving is bad, it's not, it's excellent. Using your mind analytically is fantastic, we are blessed to be able to do it, but there is a limit to what it can do and fortunately there is a whole other way to use your mind that is very beneficial, but most of us are not very good at it. Or we are good at it but we don't know we are good at it and we don't give that muscle any credit in our life. We give the credit to pushing in our life and keeping our foot on the accelerator – that gets all the credit. But when you really sit with people and you ask them, talk to me about a time when you exceeded your own expectations, talk to me about a time when you were at your best, they won't describe pushing, or figuring it out. It's just that they don't give that capacity any respect. I'm highlighting that capacity so that they go out into their life, so that they realise they have two capacities to rely on – an unbeatable combination.

Is this the end of the story?

Depends. Do they have another problem they want to solve? Hopefully what they see is the generic nature of what they just learned, the universal nature of what they just learned, it's like an all purpose cleaner, you can use it for everything! So that's what I am hoping happens. If they don't see that, for example, if they come to me with a very specific problem and they feel like they have solved it and then they ask me another very specific problem, I'll ask them how it's different from the first problem. I want to hear their answer and if they say this is totally different, then I know I have to go back to square one because they did not get the universal nature of what I was trying to point to. If they say, "Oh, oh, it's right, it's exactly the same problem!" then I know we are fine and we are done for now.

Is the feeling important for you when working with clients?

Absolutely. Mine and theirs. I'm always listening to my own feeling. I want to know what feeling I'm in when I'm working because I'm human. I can get frustrated, I can get impatient, I can get pushy, I can get critical, I can get hopeless, so I want to be awake to that because it's letting me know what's happening inside my own mind. Of course, we think it's letting us know what's wrong with the client or we think it's letting us know what's wrong with us in terms of we're not effective or we're not good enough – all of that self doubt. I want to be awake to whether or not that's happening in me and know that it's a temporary thought that I don't want to pay attention to. Waking up to it and realising what it is and where it's coming from is, generally speaking, all I need to find my centre again or to get settled again.

The good thing about working in an intensive format is that I have four whole days so if we need to take a break, we can take a break. I can suggest taking an hour-long break or taking a walk. I can do a lot of creative things that may not be possible in an hour session. As best I can, I want to reset myself, but I am also looking for my client's feeling. I have a bit of a semi-permeable membrane so that I want to let in the client's feeling enough so that I can be aware of where he or she is at and if I can't tell, I ask, "How are you feeling? What's going on?" I hear my Three Principles colleagues say this a lot, "I want to go deep with my client, I want to get in a deep feeling". That never occurs to me. I get into a deep feeling with my clients all the time, but I don't purposely do it. I don't look to do it, I'm not conscious of doing it, it just seems to happen.

People talk about a deep feeling or a beautiful feeling and Syd (Sydney Banks) used to say, look for a feeling. Would you share what that means to you?

I know that when I would listen to Syd I would get into a feeling, I would call it a deep feeling. It was a very peaceful, positive, "all-is-right-with-the-world" feeling. I think that's what happens when you hear the truth. We all know the truth, we all come from the same energy. We know truth when we hear it. It automatically settles us down. It stops the churning, the mental momentum that people live in. Me too from time to time. I want that to happen with my clients, I want the mental momentum to settle down. I want them to feel good, I want them to feel hopeful and peaceful because I think when people are peaceful and settled, they are very wise. I am aiming for that.

There is a feeling to listening beyond the intellect and I think Syd was pointing to this as well. He wanted us to notice that Listening – with an uppercase "L" – was different from listening with a lowercase "l".

Finally, I think Syd said look for a feeling because he knew that we feel our thinking. So if you were sitting in the audience listening to him speak and you were agitated, he wanted you to know what your feeling was telling you, what's going on within your mind. It's your indicator light, it's the dashboard light on your car, it's not about what Syd's saying, it's about what's happening in you.

I want my clients to look for a feeling because it's valuable information. We have misunderstood what our feelings are telling us for millennia. We thought our feelings were telling us what's happening out there, what's going right or wrong out there, what's going right or wrong with the person in front of me. But that's not what our feelings are telling us. Our feelings are telling us what's happening within. That's all they can ever tell us because that's where feelings are born, inside via thought.

I think it's exceptionally valuable to check in with your feeling. Syd would say look for a positive feeling, I think he'd say that because that's an indicator that you are in a good place and most of us want to be in a good place. I've never had anybody come to me and say, "Sandy, I think I need more depression! How about more anxiety, can you help me with that?!" Nobody has ever asked me that! They come and say they want more peace of mind, more confidence, more ease.

Looking for a positive feeling is letting you know – is your mind going to serve up what you're looking for or not? Your feeling is going to tell you. It's a very valuable resource point for all of us. I love it in a session when you feel this quiet, you feel people's minds still. I let it be if I'm doing a one-on-one, I'll just let that silence be for a while and I'll ask, "What happened? What just happened?" And it's almost always that someone just saw something that really struck them, something brand new. I'm looking for that to happen in a session.

Could you share a story or stories of what worked well and what didn't and what are the takeaways?

I think what this story illustrates is coming back to the value of listening to a client deeply before trying to teach anything.

I was seeing a woman individually, who was part of a team I had worked with previously. I noticed her in the group, she was stressed out and overwhelmed a lot of the time. I did an individual session with her and she was describing her life; her work had changed, her role had changed and she was really stressed out. She was the mother of four children (three stepchildren and her own biological daughter) and things were not going well, particularly with the 15 year old stepdaughter.

She was in a new role, it was requiring more and more of her time and she wasn't able to spend time at home and her husband was not happy – things were just coming at her from all directions. I was listening to her and she must have repeated the phrase, "I don't know why I can't figure this out", three or four times. I let her talk. She described everything that was going badly for her interspersed with, "I don't know why I can't figure this out." So finally I asked her what she meant by that particular phrase.

This is what I mean about not jumping to teach because it's so tempting at that point to say, "Oh let me tell you about what figuring it out does and how it doesn't work". It's so tempting to show her a new way right then and there. When you are deeply listening to clients I think that you get fed questions and interventions that are so much better than anything you'd ever think of. That's pretty much what happened. It occurred to me to ask her, "What is that, what does that mean?"

She proceeded to tell me that when she was in college she met the love of her life and they got married and he was her soulmate. They were married for three years, she got pregnant and they were just over the moon. When she was six months pregnant, her husband dropped dead at 31 years old, no warning, a cardiac arrest, and he just died. She explained that when it happened she was devastated and grieving, but yet there was a calmness that came over her. She was six months pregnant and needed to stay in good shape, she didn't want anything to happen to her baby. She delivered the baby and her family kept expecting her to fall apart and she never did. She told me that she was so sad, so very sad, but she knew what to do, she had clarity and now she's asking herself, "I don't know why I can't figure it out this time?"

I asked her this question, "What makes you think you figured it out the first time?" You could see in her face that I had hit on something, it was one of those silences. She asked, "What do you mean?" I answered, "What makes you think you figured it out the first time?" She said she didn't know. I explained that her mind is designed to bring her what she needs, it did it through the most difficult circumstance you can possibly imagine. "What makes you think it won't bring it to you now?"

She wanted to know why her mind wasn't helping her now and I commented on what she was doing. She did one of those eye rolls and said, "You're right, I'm just working, working all the time and all I do is think about it, all I do is try to figure it out, I try to squeeze minutes in my day". And she said, "I just can't do that, I have to let go".

We talked a little longer, but I didn't go into a long explanation because I could tell she saw something. She then decided to take three days off work, which was unheard of. If you had suggested she take three days off work she would have said there was no possible way. Now she saw she needed a break. The first day she spent walking on the beach, and she didn't think about work. She just walked. It was late fall and early winter so nobody was out there, she had the place to herself and she just walked and walked and walked. The second day she took her 15 year old stepdaughter out of school and they spent the day watching movies and eating popcorn and essentially reconnecting. The third day she made her husband take the day off and they spent the day together. After three days off she went back to work and she said, as you can imagine, she had more work than ever and yet she didn't feel stressed.

That's what I'm trying to do for people, I'm not giving them answers, I'm trying to help them see their own answers and see that their own mind is designed to give them answers. The only reason it's not is because they have fallen into a worldwide conspiracy that your circumstances can somehow make you feel a certain way. This is not possible, but we believe it's possible. We have overwhelming circumstances, we must be overwhelmed, we have a stressful job, we must be stressed, we have four kids, we must go crazy, that's what we are told. When you break that spell – no, no, no, it's not coming from the outside it's coming from inside – there's only one way our mind works – then the mind gets to give us the intelligence, the wisdom, it's been trying to give us all along while we have been on a different channel.

Chapter Three

Dicken Bettinger EdD

"The more you begin to accept yourself, the happier you become. The happier you become, the more you want to get deeper into Self. It is a journey of love because eventually it leads to pure love."
The Island of Knowledge by Linda Quiring

How do you describe the work you do with clients?

I like the word mentoring because the Principles have helped me see we are all the same and we work the same and we are being lived by the same dynamic, the same forces. Each one of us is always a student of what life can teach us. When two people get together, I used to think that one person was an expert and their job was to impart to the other person information about what they had learned. Now I see this very, very differently. True learning is when two people get together and let go of what they already know and reflect on things to see what new and fresh can be revealed to them. It's not so much that I'm the expert coach as much as I'm an intrepid fellow explorer and we are going to launch ourselves into the unknown and see what new we can see about life that seems true. I love that process, it never gets old. It's not a matter of us being experts, but rather that we are both eternal students.

As a psychologist I used to point people to what was visible; thought content, feeling content, and behaviour content. That was the entire domain of psychology. After ten years of working with this model as a psychologist I met a man named Sydney Banks. Syd had had an enlightenment experience. He realised that every moment of psychological experience that we have is created from the infinite field of energy that exists in the universe. Some people call this the spiritual dimension of life.

So now as a mentor, I remind people and point them towards the true source of their experience and how it creates every one of our thoughts, feelings, perceptions, and bodily sensations.

As a psychologist I got very interested in Syd's assertion that it's actually scientific to say there is a formless source to every psychological experience. I am discovering that it makes a huge difference where people think their experience comes from. I used to think our feelings and experiences were caused by our circumstances, other people, the past, our biology, or our genetics. Syd Banks comes along and says it appears that way, but that's not true, that's a misunderstanding. There's only one source to experience and that's the energy of life that has the capability of creating life.

That's what I see I am doing as a mentor, reminding people of what's always been true and then reflecting on it with them. It's been my experience that when people stop living in a misunderstanding, about where experience comes from, then they begin to live with an awe and appreciation for the true source of experience. What this realisation has done for me and my clients is that it straightens out our world, psychologically, very quickly. It gets harder and harder to blame our experience on the world. This helps people take ownership for their experience, take responsibility for it and it allows people to let go of an enormous amount of thinking that is creating tension, stress, or upset or simply is not necessary. And when people have less thinking, they have more clarity, they feel better, they think better and their wellbeing improves. I find that as any of us realise more deeply how our minds actually work from the inside-out that we go through life with greater ease and with more love and understanding.

What are The Three Principles?

The Three Principles, as realised by Sydney Banks, are Mind, Consciousness, and Thought. These Principles are the ultimate foundation behind all psychological functioning. They are the ultimate source of all human experience. This source could also be called pure energy, the quantum field, the life force, or the spiritual dimension of life.

Mind is the intelligence behind life that knows how to create and operate all that takes the specific forms of thinking, sensations, feelings, and behaviour. Sometimes this intelligence is called wisdom. We are all connected to that wisdom and have access to it.

Consciousness is the formless source of our capacity to be aware of life. It is what brings our senses to life. Consciousness is what allows all of us to be aware of our connection to wisdom and aware of the fact that we think and that that thinking creates what we feel.

Thought is the formless power that creates the specific feelings and experiences that we have, moment to moment. Because the Principles are formless, they are what is called the “inside” of life and our thoughts and feelings and behaviours have form so they are called the “outside” of life. The Three Principles is an inside-out paradigm that can explain all of human psychological experience. This formless core of all human beings cannot be hurt or damaged by anything that happens to us in life. It is our essence or very nature. All human beings are connected to the same essential source.

What’s the driver behind the way you work with clients? Your philosophy?

My philosophy has to do with love. As clients insightfully gain a deeper understanding of how we all actually work from the inside-out, they experience an awakening of their hearts. One time Syd Banks said that this is a journey of love that ends in pure love. It allows us to begin to feel more and more connected in a life-affirming positive way with other people and with nature.

When I very first got exposed to the Principles I became so much more compassionate and understanding toward my kids who were 8 and 13 at the time. I immediately began to take ownership for my reaction to my kids. I wasn't blaming them and thinking I had to change them so that I could feel better. This completely changed my understanding of what it meant to be a parent. It allowed me to become more relaxed in parenting, more understanding, more compassionate and to feel more and more love for my own kids. This also became true with my wife and then with my clients. How wonderful I could learn something and share this with others and watch them fall in love with others and with life. Syd says it's a different kind of love because it's not directed toward just a person or a particular object, it's directed towards the whole world. It's unconditional love. I think my whole life that's the only thing I've really been interested in. The question I most asked Syd was, "Okay Syd, can you talk some more about love?" This remains my primary interest. I love seeing people wake up at the heart! There is nothing more rewarding for me as a human being than to see that happen.

If there was one thing you could tell your younger self about working with clients, what would it be?

It was what I kept telling my kids, everything you feel is okay, there are no bad feelings.

Your insecurity and stress and upset are normal, but it is important to understand where these feelings come from. When you know they are created from inside of you, by your own thinking, then you won't be frightened of any of those feelings. They'll come and go much more naturally. You will be more resilient. Understanding how our experience is created via thought takes away a lot of the misunderstanding about feelings. We stop blaming our upset feelings on other people and the world and we stop looking for the world to make us feel better. I couldn't wait to share that with my kids. When I was able to share it in a way they could hear and when they were open to it, boy did that make a difference in their lives. They got intrigued by the fact that it was thought in the moment that was creating all of our feelings.

The other thing I wanted to share with them was that we all already have everything we are looking for. We already have perfect wellbeing inside of us. We already have peace, joy and love inside and that the only thing that covers up our wellbeing is our own thinking. When all of our personal thinking quiets down then feelings of wellbeing naturally arise in us. This fact can be seen in ourselves and others over and over again. I told my kids that when their heads cleared of upsetting thoughts that they would naturally feel good and have all the common sense they needed to deal with whatever their friends were doing, whatever was happening in school, however teachers treated them. I told them that this understanding would allow them access to feelings that uplift and contain all the common sense they needed to guide them through all the challenges that come their way.

So those are the two things I would want my younger self to know; where my feelings came from – I didn't learn that until I was in my forties – I sure could have benefited from that when I was little, especially in high school, oh my gosh I was insecure. And I would want my younger self to know you have perfect wellbeing inside but for your thinking. That's such a hopeful message. It's a beautiful message I have enjoyed sharing with lots of young people.

Do you prepare for a client session and if so, how?

I have to say I love preparing for anything. For me, preparing is not something special. I prepare constantly. Here's what I mean by preparing though. For me preparing is letting go of everything I think and relaxing – just being – and then new ideas occur to me. I want to be that way all the time, not just before I meet with a client. It looks like preparing, but it's funny because you are not preparing for the future, but you're preparing for this moment. Opening myself up to what is new and fresh. That's what some people call preparing. So if I'm meeting with a client, I might in a quiet, reflective moment, get ideas of something to ask them or I'll remember something they've said that I'm curious about. It could also be that I remember something they've said that, later on, becomes very helpful in our discussion, or a metaphor that they've used and I see a really clear way to build on their metaphor so that it will help them better understand something. To me it's being open and reflective to the new and fresh.

It's the direction more and more that I'm living my life. My wife started telling me about a year ago, she said, "Dicken, you really do what you talk about with clients because I see you so often in the day just dis-engage completely from your intellect, resting in the now and getting renewed. I can see when you are feeling tense or stressed or upset that that's the first place you go. That didn't used to be the case. I used to see you when things weren't going well. You would think much harder about your life and now it's the opposite, you think less when you are stressed and open to the new. I see how it's your go-to-place".

Syd started calling that place the state of no thought. He said it doesn't mean you don't have thoughts but you're not paying attention to the content of your thinking as it flows through your mind. He said over and over that we go beyond all concepts to this state of no thought to find what we are looking for. Sometimes he called this state pure consciousness.

Pure consciousness is any moment of awareness that's free of the contamination of our conceptual mind. He said that pure consciousness is what every human being is looking for because the instant we step beyond our intellect and touch that space of pure consciousness that something new and fresh must come in. This deeper intelligence, which he often called wisdom, knows how to bring in feelings that are uplifting and helpful to us in the moment and thoughts that are helpful in terms of responding well to whatever is going on in front of us. Wisdom is a responsive intelligence that brings us exactly what we need in a very practical way. So all I need to do is to have the faith that if I let go of everything I know and step into the unknown, that it's going to be a responsive unknown. So we begin to have more trust and faith in wisdom. He realised that the essence of Mind is the intelligence behind all life. Syd said that when we surrender our personal thinking wisdom will reveal its secrets to us.

What's your intention with a client, if any? Are you trying to get them to see anything?

No. When I meet with a client I don't want to have any intention because that becomes an agenda. I want to be wide open to what wisdom brings new and fresh in response to whatever they say and so I'm hesitant to try to hold on to an intention to do anything. Wisdom will bring to mind what's helpful or it wouldn't be called wisdom – I don't know what it would be called, stupidity or something – but it's wisdom! It will bring to mind what's helpful and responsive to anything a person says to us or to any circumstance we find ourselves in.

I learned to recognise the difference between having an agenda in my mind when I'm with someone and when I meet them with no agenda. I don't have to worry about sharing with them what I know about the Principles because wisdom will bring that to mind if it is helpful. When we meet someone with nothing on our minds, then we get rapport with them and then at some point things occur to us to say to share with them. I've noticed when I'm with someone at some point what I know to be true comes to mind to share with people. I don't have to have an intention about that, wisdom knows what it's doing, so the more I get out of the way the better it works out. I keep learning that lesson over and over again.

Remember I said that there were two things I'd tell my younger self? The first is that all your experience is thought created, and the second is that you can rely on wisdom. You can trust wisdom. The two of those together, if you see the true nature of feelings and where they come from and if you have faith and trust in wisdom, those two awaken a greater sense of connection to life in a life-affirming, positive way. It awakens our hearts, it awakens love.

One time Syd said that the feeling of love and the state of no thought are coupled together like lovers. Oh I like that. Syd would say listen for a feeling because if you really listen you have to let go of everything you are thinking. To really listen you have a moment where you disengage with the intellect – all your ideas and concepts – which leaves you wide open and receptive. And then you begin to feel more alive and connected to others and to life. That's my experience. I've loved really reflecting on that, and looking into that and it seems like no matter what I'm feeling, when I fall out of all of my ideas and concepts then that feeling will open up and expand. That's a nice feeling. So anger that's not limited by concept begins to radiate and it feels like determination and purpose as opposed to personal. I had the insight that all feelings are love in disguise.

Is there a process to your client work? Components?

Not that I can figure out. I think wisdom creates its own process so if I'm relying upon wisdom it's different every time. If I try to create a process then I stop listening for wisdom and I just follow an idea and sort of get set in my direction. So I like the process that wisdom reveals to me when I work with people. It's beautiful, really beautiful, because it keeps moving both of us deeper and deeper into reflection and closer to truth and awakens this deeper feeling of aliveness, connection, understanding, compassion. That's quite a process! Wisdom knows what it's doing. It knows how to move us in that direction.

What happens within you if you get into trouble with a client, what do you do?

I don't see it as trouble, I get lost like anybody else – I get caught up in my thinking in a way that I don't listen very well or I don't see something. I innocently block my access to love and wisdom. At some point I'm bound to realise that and then I can come back, apologise to the client and say, "Listen, I was just thinking too hard about something and I didn't really get what you were trying to say, could you say it again?" What I love about the Principles is that at any moment rather than beating yourself up for getting lost, you can be grateful that you caught yourself and get a fresh start. Wisdom will then help you make amends or help you get back on track and that's just a natural part of any relationship, and certainly in a mentoring relationship.

How do you know you have got lost?

I think as our understanding deepens, we get more and more sensitive to tension as a signal that we are misusing the intellect. We are caught in the intellect and we've stopped being open to wisdom. That's what I mean by getting lost. It's like Syd saying if you REALLY see thought creating an insecure or uncomfortable feeling, that seeing will bring you right back to the now. Here we are again in the now, open and receptive to wisdom helping us take the next step. I think we get more sensitive to the signals that alert us that we are lost. It's like an alarm clock going off. At first when I learned the Principles the alarm had to be so loud it was like screaming. Now a little tinkle, a little bell, a little bit of tension gives me a signal. For example, I'm talking to someone and maybe I feel a little impatient. That's a common one for me – to feel a little impatient. If I don't see that, then I don't listen very well when I'm impatient. I interrupt or I talk over and that still happens. But if I feel impatient and I see that as an alarm, or an indicator that I am getting lost, then I wake back up to the now and get a fresh start.

I love this notion that if we really see thought, that it brings you right back to the now. When we are in the now there is no technique and we don't have to do anything, no matter what personal thinking we were caught up in. When we are in the now, any personal thinking just begins to melt away naturally. In other words, we can't sustain reactive feeling and thinking if we are in the now. That's where our thinking and feeling begins to flow and it always passes and we become more resilient. If I don't see it right away, at some point I will. I want people to know I'm human and normal and I'm no different than they are and at times I get caught up in my thinking. I lose sight of the spiritual nature of life, lose sight of wisdom. Clients appreciate that kind of honesty and openness. They are glad to know that they don't really have to put you on a pedestal and that you are human too. We are all in the same boat here, it's a level playing field, I like that.

Did you put Syd on a pedestal?

At times we all did, but he was very good at knocking himself off the pedestal. If he couldn't get us to take him off the pedestal, he would suddenly show up in a way that was hard to put him on a pedestal (laughing).

He wasn't all love and light all the time?

I often think of babies being very comfortable with having whatever experience they are having because they are in the preconceptual stage so that they don't have shoulds, and they don't have judgment, so they just feel what they feel. Syd was like that. He wasn't at all what I imagined an enlightened human being to be like. He was so comfortable feeling what he was feeling without judging.

What about the people around him? If he was angry?

At first a lot of us would get unnerved. Then over time it got easier and easier to be okay with whatever he was feeling and to be okay with whatever we were feeling. Understanding allowed us to be less frightened of our own feelings and the feelings of others. In other words, we become less insecure in the face of other people's feelings. At a certain point sometimes it would appear as if Syd was getting upset and going after our egos, full bore. Those who knew Syd would advise others that if Syd goes after your ego that you are fortunate, and to not take it personally. We tried to help each other. In the same way my wife and I would say that to our kids, listen, your Mom's not in a great mood right now, don't take it personally. We started doing that with Syd too and we learned from that. We learned not to get into our thinking about someone else's experience. That was really helpful.

With understanding, people are freer to have feelings. I feel my feelings way more directly than I ever used to, but with understanding you're less inclined to get stuck in them or to act on them. It's like when people have colds, they can be okay with the fact that they sneeze without thinking that it's a good idea to run up to somebody and sneeze in their face. This is what I see happens psychologically, people become okay with the fact that they have a wide range of emotions, and with understanding, they become less inclined to sneeze that emotion in somebody's face. As Syd would say, they wouldn't bring that thinking to life by acting on it. It's really powerful to be wide open and accepting of all experience and having the wisdom and understanding to know when to act and when not to act. At higher levels of understanding we feel our feelings more directly, but we are less inclined to act on them in a way that isn't helpful or loving or respectful.

The more comfortable we get when we are upset, the easier it is for people to be around us. When we are uncomfortable, people tend to get uncomfortable. I like thinking that as we understand the Principles more, the purpose is not to be in a good mood all the time, the purpose is to get more at ease with going through the inevitable ups and downs that we go through. So we get more comfortable with getting more uncomfortable.

Is problem solving for a client the end of the story? Or do you go further?

For me problem solving is not the beginning or the end. I don't work to try and help people solve problems. If people jump to a higher level of consciousness, most problems disappear or they are not problems any more. I'm way more interested in people waking up to how the mind works and the true nature of the mind. I could just say I'm more interested in them waking up to their true selves because I know that that is the answer to all their problems, so rather than look at problems and try and solve them, I help people find what resolves all problems.

Syd would say that love is always, always, the answer. It's like whenever I have a problem, if I look outside and start thinking about the problem or people or the situation, I get more lost, I get more drawn into the story. If, when I feel like there is a problem, I wake up out of my personal thinking and fall into this inner, quieter space, then wisdom brings me feelings that lift my spirits and the quality of my thinking improves. That's the answer every time to what I'm looking for. When I'm feeling love in my heart it doesn't seem like life is a problem to be solved. It's an opportunity to bring more love and understanding into the world.

Is the feeling important for you when working with clients?

Understanding allows us to be in any experience and there is a feeling of understanding. It's different from what I used to think. I used to want to be in a good feeling and so I would be expending energy trying to be in a good feeling and not liking when I wasn't in a good feeling.

With understanding I can be with any feeling when I'm with a client, but I don't collapse into my personal feeling the way that I used to. When I don't feel good, if I fall out of my personal thinking, if I let go of my personal thinking, wisdom will always bring a helpful response, regardless of what mood I'm in. There is a feeling to that but it's a much bigger feeling of; understanding, of knowing, of accepting, of allowing, of openness, of presence that can embrace the full range of human experience – that's the feeling.

I thought you were going to say love!

That is love. My description of love has changed. I can be in a low mood and if I'm living with an understanding it just means that even while I'm in a low mood I'm not wedded to my thinking so that something new and fresh can come through. When our minds are open and receptive we feel more connected to others in a good way. That's love. I can be in a low mood and be very kind and loving, this has been a mind blower for me. I don't have to wait until I'm in a better feeling. I used to spend half my life waiting for my moods to pass so I could be loving. And then I found out that if I'm in a low mood and caught up in my conceptual mind, then wisdom doesn't break through and I'm not very kind hearted. If I'm in a low mood and I drop out of my intellect, then I can still be in a low mood and be kind.

I recently spent a lot of time in the hospital, I had three major operations and I went through an enormous amount of pain. I saw that when I was caught up in my personal thinking I wasn't very kind, I was very introverted, I was in my ego. When I would wake up to the fact of thought it would throw me back into the now and I'd still have pain, but spontaneously I would start being kind to the nurses or to anybody who was in the room, like my wife. It was a love that was not dependent upon specific feelings or circumstances. It's a deeper love, it's a more unconditional love that can embrace any feeling and any mood, it's an unconditional love.

Could you share a story or stories of what worked well and what didn't and what are the takeaways for you?

In that sense, every client I work with is a story, every single client is a story. We're all the same. A client shows up and they're having a lot of experiences that they attribute to something other than thought. Well that's suffering. The good news is we all suffer because we all have experiences that we attribute to something other than thought, other than being created from within. Everybody. The good news is that it's built into us to be aware of how that works.

I love that every client is a story, a story of waking up to what's always been true but that they didn't realise was true. This happened to me for the very first time when I was at my first training in the Principles. I was in my hotel room thinking about something that was going to happen a week later and I was getting very anxious. Then, for the first time I realised in the moment that I was thinking up anxiety. I asked myself, why am I thinking about this if it's making me anxious? Immediately, I knew, I *knew* it wasn't helpful. As soon as I saw the fact that I was feeling thought, I came back to the now and I felt better. From then on I started catching myself all over the place worrying, thinking up anxiety.

Understanding took away a huge percentage of my worry very quickly. Almost overnight it took away perhaps 60% of my worry. That's huge! If you have a backpack that weighs 100 pounds and you take off 60 pounds, then going up the mountain gets a lot easier. That was the very first story about this that I could tell clients. This was my first story of waking up to the fact of thought in the moment and how that realisation freed me up from a lot of unnecessary thinking that was weighing on me.

The next story was with my kids in parenting. I went home from the first training and I kept waking up to the fact of thought. I started to realise how much it made a difference in what feeling I was bringing to my kids. And then I realised that I could be a really phenomenal parent if I didn't keep bringing annoyance, bother, upset, impatience, and judgments to my kids. No wonder parenting seemed difficult. All I had to do was to be aware of my own state of mind and be particular about my feelings. That realisation changed my parenting very quickly.

As I better understood the fact of thought, I began to see that when I got upset with my wife she didn't have anything to do with it – my feeling was not because of her but a reflection of my own thinking. It got easier for me to get over being upset when it was just thought. That was the second story that I could share with my clients.

I had 30 clients as a psychologist. I'd been working for ten years and when I returned from my first training in the Principles, I started introducing them to the fact that thought creates reality. Unbelievable.

One couple came into my office and they had been fighting every single day. You know why they came to see me? To get better at fighting! They wanted to learn how to fight fair. They couldn't even imagine that they could deal with their differences without fighting. They assumed it was a natural part of life and they had to learn how to get better at it. I spent ten minutes talking to them about when any of us realises that our upset is created by our own thinking, that thinking falls away and the feeling changes when our thinking changes. I told them that when my head cleared that it was much easier to deal with my wife when I was in a calmer state of mind. During the first session they were sitting at opposite ends of the room. They came into the second session and sat side by side and were holding hands. They were all lovey dovey and I said, "Oh wow, what happened?" They said that they had had an amazing week, that they didn't even have a single fight! They said, "Don't get us wrong, we did get upset, but when we realised it was just thought, we got over it pretty quickly and then we would come back together after we got over our upset". They told me they had some amazing talks, way better than they had before and that they were working stuff out and it was going great. I worked with this couple that had been so unhappy for only three sessions. When they understood better where their feelings were really coming from, they were off and running with a whole new basis for their relationship.

I love that every person that has an insight into the Principles becomes a teaching story. That it shows how we're all the same. We can all wake up to the fact of thought and it takes the blame out of our experience in our relationships and we can all experience greater wellbeing when we touch that space within, that Syd called pure consciousness. When we open into that space, something new and fresh comes in. The fact that everybody can experience this truth is so hopeful. We experience for ourselves how wisdom moves us towards love and understanding. It's designed to do that. When our personal thinking falls away wisdom guides us toward thriving, but we don't have to take anybody's word for it, we need to see if that is true for ourselves.

Chapter Four

Gabriela Maldonado-Montano

"Throughout time, human beings have experienced insights that spontaneously and completely changed their behavior and their lives, bringing them happiness they previously had thought impossible."
The Missing Link by Sydney Banks

What are The Three Principles?

The Three Principles are the most fundamental laws or building blocks of the human experience and they are at work every moment of our lives whether we are aware of them or not. These Principles are present in our work and in our personal lives. One of the most helpful and practical benefits of these building blocks is that they transcend culture, religion, politics, educational level, gender identity, genetics, biology, etc. Mind, Thought and Consciousness are at the base of every human being.

Mind – is the fountain of LIFE. It is the energy and intelligence that creates all things and people. It is the origin of creativity, genius, resourcefulness and insight. It is present even when it is not obvious to us.

Thought – comes from Mind as a creative agent to experience the world. It is constant, and ever changing. It is never stagnant and it has a diverse expression. Sometimes this Principle is visible to us but lots of times it is completely invisible.

Consciousness – a "branch" of Mind as well, brings to light Mind and Thought. It gifts us our feeling state and ability to discover the breath of Life. It offers us a navigation system to move through life.

How do you describe the work you do with clients?

I have dedicated my entire professional life to help my clients discover the wellbeing and natural genius that resides at the centre of their being and to understand the fundamental laws that create the human experience so they can navigate through their lives with more ease, gentleness and joy. This work takes many forms such as coaching, facilitating group trainings, mentoring and developing topic specific programmes to mention some. Whatever the form, the goal is always to help people understand how they function at the most fundamental level so they can thrive.

What's the driver behind the way you work with clients? Your philosophy?

Understanding the Principles, the laws of nature that govern my psychology and spirituality, has allowed me to live life with a sense of kindness, grace and possibility. I am profoundly grateful for the gift of understanding and I want to share it with others. My driving force is the possibility that exists for all of us to live life with a sense of gentleness and hope. Feeling supported by LIFE is an awesome experience.

At the centre of my commitment and desire is the realisation that all of us belong to LIFE (aka Spirit, Life Force, Mind). Wanting to share this, not only with words and client work but in my daily life, feels like a natural extension of this realisation. In the movie Avatar there is a line that one of the characters tells another that illustrates this beautifully: "I SEE YOU."

I have been with hundreds of people during times of struggle, in situations that were challenging. Being able to SEE them in spite of their current circumstances, feeling states, past experiences or behaviours, cuts through limitations. It directs me to a quality of working with clients (accompanying, listening, asking questions, sharing, discovering, pointing, teaching) that allows them not to get entangled in the details of their stories. I have been present with many clients as they were experiencing insights that brought them a sense of possibility. Every single time this happens is touching and beautiful; it reinforces my commitment to continue to work this way.

If there was one thing you could tell your younger self about working with clients, what would it be?

There are two pieces of advice I would give myself: look at this understanding to see how it plays out in your life both in the ordinary and the extraordinary; and don't try so hard.

One of the comments that Sydney Banks made over and over again was to be selfish with this understanding: "At first, look at this understanding for your own life rather than for the purpose of helping someone else." This made a lot of sense to me. I have reminded myself often that this is a journey of personal discovery first. SEEING how the human experience gets created and how "real" it can feel regardless of the specifics allows me to experience compassion, patience and acceptance of my current state of mind. I have felt humbled many times.

Keeping an eye on my own personal journey has been super, super helpful. It is very interesting to see the impact this has in my work. It has become easier to see the Principles in action (resilience, insight, creation of experience) even when clients are sharing compelling circumstances. I notice that the quality of my listening is deeper and quieter which allows me to be more present, this creates an environment of calmness and serenity that my clients can benefit from immediately.

The other thing that has impacted my coaching tremendously was the shift I had around trying too hard. In hindsight, I appreciate why this happened – it was an honest misunderstanding on my part. Let me explain.

Understanding the Principles impacted my life profoundly in every area. Personally, I went to my first training with Dr Roger Mills at a time when I was going through a divorce and thought I would die of the pain. Hearing Roger say, "There is a part of you that is untouchable regardless of what has happened in your past or your current circumstances", awoke me to a truth I recognised in my soul.

Professionally, I had the great fortune of teaching classes and facilitating groups for the Department of Alcohol and Drug Services in the County of Santa Clara in California starting in 1996. Our mission was to share the Principles with the residents of this county. Today, I recognise that I became a little too eager. I had the agenda of trying to share the Principles with whoever would listen, actually whoever was in front of me. I dismissed colleagues that worked differently from me because I was trying to share the power of the Principles. I was trying to convince people that understanding the Principles could save the world in the same way that it saved me. When I encountered resistance I thought they were stubborn and were not listening ... sometimes I tried harder.

At that time, I did not see that these laws had functioned perfectly from the beginning of time. That my innocent "pushing-it-down-the-throat-approach", filled with urgency, was blind to the depth and breadth of these universal laws. The power is not in the words but something beyond them – as Syd said so many times.

Do you prepare for a client session and if so, how?

I like to have some quiet time before every session. A few minutes of silence serve as a bridge to get my mind still, to become more present. My hope is to be as present as possible for my clients.

The most powerful preparation I have found is my daily life. I realised, some time ago, that I have an opportunity to see the Principles in action, to learn how to listen deeper, and to see psychological innocence in every moment of my life. Just recently I was reflecting on an experience with someone in my life for whom I tend to have lots of judgment. During a particular time, I felt my opinion of this person was a "fact" and lots of evidence came to mind to support it. At some point I started to notice the strength and quality of my emotions – my righteousness. Then, I had a moment of stillness followed by compassion. At some point in my life I have learned to look at these experiences as opportunities to SEE the universality of the human experience.

Later on that week as I was having a session with one of my clients, I noticed the same thing was happening to her. She was seeing her opinions as "facts" and was stating the evidence to support her belief. Her feelings were strong. She could not see the Principles in action in this situation in the same way that I couldn't see the Principles in action earlier in the week. I felt a sense of compassion for my client. Life feels intense at times. I did not consider the all too popular, "Can you see how this is your thinking?" question. I noticed that my listening got quieter. A question arose in my mind: "Do you want to see something new about this particular situation?" Her answer was, "Yes".

Noticing my own psychology in action, at a universal level, prepares me to notice it in my clients. It helps me to not get entangled with the details of their story: it confirms the capacity people have to experience insight at any moment, it allows me to listen deeper and above all it lets me accompany my clients in their journey of life with care and compassion.

What's your intention with a client, if any? Are you trying to get them to see anything?

My initial intention is to offer my client an environment where he or she feels listened to; feels able to share whatever is on his or her mind freely, to feel free of judgments, to feel free of any agenda and not feel shame of his or her experience of life.

These qualities create an environment of acceptance, freedom and openness which allows both of us to be present and to listen from stillness. Often when people are present, they are able to experience a shift in perspective and see something new. I often use their insights to showcase their own wisdom, resilience, and capacity for insight.

During sessions, I often notice things they haven't realised about their psychological functioning, or misunderstandings, that make their life experience difficult. At this time my intention is to share this understanding, but above all my intention is to be of service.

Is there a process to your client work? Components?

At this point in my career, working with clients feels natural and fluid. There are, however, components that have to do with my own understanding which feel "invisible", but that drive more visible components that show up as guidelines. They work hand in hand. Please keep in mind that this is just a way for me to express a process that is more like art and less like a recipe.

Some time ago, I REALISED that every client I work with is Mind, Consciousness and Thought in action. This has become fundamental in my work and has allowed me to see my clients as partners. I enter each session with a great sense of respect and alliance.

SEEING this allows me to recognise the essence in my clients in spite of their circumstances or past experiences, which helps me to be present and listen from stillness. It is common for me to be in awe of my clients' wisdom and their ability to have insight around their own functioning. I've noticed the feeling of presence and stillness offers them a lot of space to explore and reflect.

I KNOW it is possible for my clients to have insight at any moment, even in the most compelling of circumstances, I have witnessed this very many times. Having certainty about this human ability helps me to hang out with them in the unknown, which is the "place" where questions or sharing points arise. I like to ask permission before I start sharing – sometimes it is implied.

I use the feeling as a barometer to see how things are progressing but I also ask my clients what is resonating for them and what is making sense. Their feedback will let me know if there are any adjustments we need to make.

What happens within you if you get into trouble with a client? What do you do?

Usually, it calls my attention and stops me in my tracks. I lean on listening to discover what went wrong. Often I feel neutral about the situation and realise that stillness is the best "place" for me to be. Sometimes I get insecure or become a bit stubborn, but noticing my feeling state helps me to get reoriented to presence. When I am present, I am able to be of service again.

At the beginning of my career I had an experience that was the most intense situation I have ever been in with a client, talk about getting in trouble! I was teaching a mandated parenting class which I felt uncomfortable teaching because I do not have children. As a matter of fact my worst nightmare was that the participants would find out – and it happened, but only ten times worse than in my dreams. One day a Dad started yelling at me, he told me, “Easy for you to say and what do you know anyway, you do not even have children!” He stood up from his chair and was screaming in front of the entire class. By the grace of God I was calm through the entire episode. My listening was very still and I did not feel attacked. As I was listening to him something occurred to me that helped him calm down and we developed a nice connection. For the rest of his time in the class, he was engaged in conversation and expressed gratitude for being part of the group.

Is problem solving for a client the end of the story? Or do you go further?

The presenting problem gets taken care of and more. As my client and I embark in exploration we discover possibilities not only for the particular situation that brought them to want to work with me, but for other situations in other areas of their lives. Just recently, I was working with an executive team of a company with the purpose of enhancing their leadership. The topic of listening from stillness was coined in one of these sessions and we talked at length about its impact in the working environment. During a break one of the participants shared with me the importance of listening from stillness in his personal life – he was very touched. I could tell by his comments that he had heard something transformative for his life.

I work with people wanting to offer them an understanding that is universal and sustainable. Our work together offers them the possibility of finding solutions for the presenting problem and often they report changes in other parts of their lives.

Is the feeling important for you when working with clients?

Understanding the value of our feeling state is essential. Early on in my work with incarcerated youth a young lady told me: "We don't care what you know until we know that you care!" The feeling of her delivery was raw and strong, it stopped me in my tracks immediately. The kids I worked with during this period of time were very astute and "would call me out" when my feeling was off. If I came in with an agenda and was not present, they could tell. If one of the girls needed to be listened to and I didn't realise it, they would tell me. And when the feeling of presence and love was in the room, they could also tell.

The feeling state of a person, the tone of a conversation, the mood of a class are all indicators we can use to help us in our work and our personal lives. It is the most visible indicator I have to see what is going on inside. If a client goes from upset to peace, I know we are moving in the right direction, even if he or she can't explain it with words. If a class suddenly goes into a lot of resistance, I know I have to stop and find out what happened. If I am in a meeting and we are going around in circles and people are "digging in their heels", a break might be necessary.

The feeling is also a great indicator to let me know what is going on inside of me. I have been in client sessions and realised I am experiencing judgment. Noticing this in the moment helps me get back to the present. Understanding the value and role the feeling state has in our personal and professional life is super helpful.

Could you share a story or stories of what worked well and what didn't and what are the takeaways?

I'm working with a young mother, who shows up in a rough and intense way to her family. She was referred to me by a family member that described her as having learning problems, a temper and being very stubborn. When I first met her I encountered a lovely human being with a capacity to have a beautiful feeling. During one of our first sessions she shared the following: "I just want to provide my children with a stable home."

I couldn't understand what was going on. How come there was such a difference between some of the problem behaviour which she acknowledged, and how she was in our sessions? Something wasn't making sense to me. I LISTENED. As she continued to share I had a sense that she worried about everything. I asked her if she experienced a lot of worry and she responded: "YES, I worry constantly." We discovered that a lot of her behaviour came from worry and not from the "fact" that she was a violent, irrational human being with a learning problem.

To me this is a story of success because we discovered that her behaviour was a result of her state of mind, not a character flaw. She didn't have to worry about having to fight or control something that was part of her and she could understand the impact that worry had in her behaviour. She could relax. We continue to have deep conversations although some "problem behaviours" still arise. It is hopeful to see that she can have powerful insights in spite of having certain behaviours. She has a beautiful presence and her psychological functioning is becoming more obvious to her.

What did not work so well with this client was trying to solve a violence problem. When the family first related her behavioural problems I innocently created an image of a violent woman. There was lots of evidence.

The greatest takeaway is the importance of not assuming the origin of the presenting problem. It's easy to have a client with certain behaviours, create assumptions about them and believe those assumptions. It's very helpful to come to every single session empty minded with an attitude of discovery and offer to listen from stillness.

Chapter Five

Linda Pransky

"If the only thing that people learned was not to be afraid of their experience, that alone would change the world."
Sydney Banks

What does coaching from the Three Principles or being a Three Principles coach mean to you as in the definition?

I help people understand how their mind works, to set them free of the prison of their own thinking, and reconnect to their mental health that they were born with.

I think a good way to look at it is to contrast it with what a lot of people do in the coaching and therapeutic fields and that is that they dwell and concentrate on the content of a person's thinking. I'm not particularly interested in the content of a person's thinking because the problem is that they identify with the content of their thinking and that's what gets them into trouble. So, part of my definition would be that I, as a Three Principles coach, look to show people that they are the thinker and they generate content. A lot of the content that they generate, they can't help. It just pops into their head. But they do have something to say about how they identify with it. That's where people get into a problem, they identify with some really bad thinking, like "I'm a loser" or "I'm a bad person" or "I'm a frightened person", and they can identify with that in a very negative way. The problem isn't that they have negative thinking, the problem is that they identify with it and then they struggle with it. They try to change their experience. They try to think it away. They try to push it away and that just creates more of the experience they don't want.

Another way of defining a Three Principles Coach would be showing people their misunderstanding about their relationship with thought and who they think they are because they are the thinker not the content. What I'm looking for when working with people, and this sounds kind of corny, is to set them free from the boundaries of thought. You see people dwell in the content. They try to change the content. They try to get new boundaries and I say, "No, you don't want boundaries". **Thought is a tool not a prison.** That's what Syd taught me; **thought is a tool not a prison**. You don't have to be defined by the content. You don't have to be imprisoned by the content. You don't have to agree with the content. You don't have to do anything with the content. You don't have to fight with the content because, in fact, your experience is transient if you allow it to be transient. I don't know if I defined myself as a practitioner in the way you are looking for, but that's how I think about it.

People come to a coach because they want help. They don't realise what they need help with is their thinking. For example, people have expectations and disappointments. They don't even realise expectations and disappointments are thought. They don't realise they set themselves up for so-called problems because they set up expectations with the consequence of disappointment.

I suppose a very simple definition of a coach would be to show clients that what they are up against is thought and they can think again. They can think again.

Expectations limit people, "I expect this, I expect that". They get stuck in the expectations and they don't see what else there is. To show people what they are up against is thought and that they can think again, would be a simple definition of what a coach would do.

What's the driver behind the way you work with clients? Your philosophy?

My philosophy is based on my personal understanding of the Three Principles: my personal understanding of Consciousness, my personal understanding of Thought, and my personal understanding of Mind. What I mean by my personal understanding is the extent that I realise the truth of those Principles. That's my driver. It's my grounding in the Principles, not my intellectual understanding, but my experiential understanding where I realise, "Oh that's Thought, oh that's Consciousness, oh that's Mind". Now that said, an understanding or a grounding of Mind, Thought and Consciousness is infinite. It's not like you get there. There's no there. It's an evolution of understanding about those Three Principles, so everybody is on that continuum of evolution and people's grounding is more or less.

Syd (Sydney Banks), in my mind, realised the whole thing. Another way of saying it is, I think Syd was enlightened. I'm not enlightened, but I have a piece of it. I have a bit of it, enough to help myself and other people get some freedom around thought, and some understanding around what Thought, Mind and Consciousness means. My driver is my understanding. My driver is my grounding. My driver is my personal truth of what the Principles mean to me.

Does this make sense?

Yes it does and I see there are differences to other answers I've had so far.

It's different, but you will see the same thread.

Yes, and there appears to be no right way?

There is a right way in the sense that you teach from your grounding. Some people don't understand grounding and they teach from their intellect. If you teach from your intellect, you're not going to get results and you're not going to get clients because there is no impact. The impact comes from the feeling and the feeling comes from your understanding, which I call grounding. So, you have to teach for impact and that's from grounding. But everyone is going to teach it in their own words and in their own way. And that is okay.

There is a right way and that's teaching from your own understanding. That's what I learned from Syd. When he asked me to teach, I asked, "teach what Syd?" He said, "Teach what you know, not what you think, but what you know". I said, "I don't know very much" and he said, "It doesn't matter. You always want to teach what you know, not what you think". Well

I could give you an example of what I knew, I realised that my moods were thought. I knew that, I *knew*. I had a realisation. I knew it was thought. It's not the boogie man. It's not God punishing me. It's not something coming at me from outside via another person. My mood is thought. That set me free. That was my grounding. That was my personal thought and that was my teaching. So, there is a right way. Teach from grounding and understanding, not from the intellect, which has no impact.

Teaching and coaching - do you see any difference between the two?

No, not in my mind. Maybe in another person's mind, but not in my mind.

If there was one thing you could tell your younger self about working with clients, what would it be?

All you have to do is listen to people. Get everything off your mind and listen and tell them what you know. Not what you think, but what you know, your wisdom about life, and what you know to be true. Everybody knows something that's true. It's so simple, people know things and when they listen that knowing gets pulled out. Just listen and your wisdom will get pulled out of you. Simple matters. Truth, knowing and wisdom is simple.

When you listen and your wisdom gets pulled out of you it wakes up the wisdom in your clients and it pulls it out of them. What I didn't appreciate is that my clients had wisdom too. Once they hooked into it, they solved their own problems.

For example, you might be listening to somebody and they keep saying how much they should be doing this or how much they should be doing that and how much they have to do that. If you are listening it might occur to you to say, "What is the purpose of should and why does it matter that you follow your 'should'?" That could put your client in a reflective mind, and they could see they no longer have to be ruled by the thinking of should. Something so simple can open a world of new understanding for someone. Listen and listen deeply and say what occurs to you. If you listen deeply enough your wisdom will get pulled out. This is an example of breaking the boundaries of thought.

Do you prepare for a client session and if so, how?

Sometimes I do and sometimes I don't. It depends on what occurs to me. Usually I just turn up and listen. After I've listened in the first session, in between sessions things will occur to me about the client and I'll just sit with what occurs to me in a way that prepares me for the next session. It's not something I do, it's something that happens. I don't think about it and analyse it. Usually something puzzling will occur to me about that first session and I'll reflect on that puzzlement.

What's your intention with a client, if any? Are you trying to get them to see anything?

Sometimes my intention is to get them to see that they are caught up in thought and to get them to see that and understand that. Other times my intention is to help them see that they are not broken, there is nothing wrong with them. So many people think there is something wrong with them. They are human. They have human frailty and because they have human frailty, they think there is something wrong with them. Well, no. Everyone has human frailty. Some people take that experience too much to heart and they think they are broken. When people feel they are broken it's just that they are caught up in their thinking. They're not broken, their consciousness isn't broken. People are conscious beings. You can never break consciousness. It just appears to be broken because of the way they think and if they understand that, they realise they are not broken.

It's all about getting the client to realise something, not think something new, but to realise something true. **Not think something new, realise something true!** I want them to realise something true and realising something true is just another way of talking about understanding.

I really see the role of the practitioner is to get people to understand what they are up against. They're up against themselves. They're up against thought. That's what they're up against. They're up against thought and they fight their experience and they believe in their experience. Then they just get wrapped around the axle and they don't know it. That's the problem, they don't know it. Once they know it, people know what to do. They know how to help themselves. Once they know what they are up against they know how to help, they can generalise it and help themselves. They get wrapped up and they realise, "Oh I'm just wrapped up in my thinking", and they learn to back up, back away, and unwind.

Once you help them understand and set them free, they become their own teacher, they become their own counsel, and they don't need people to help them anymore. They start to see and feel what getting wrapped up in thought means and they learn to get out from underneath it.

Is there a process to your client work? Components?

I show up, stop thinking about myself, listen to the client and trust what occurs to me. Another way of saying that is show up, be in service, and listen. You can't be thinking about yourself when you are working with people. What I mean by thinking about yourself is: "How am I doing? Do they like what I'm saying? Is what I'm saying good? Am I getting through? Time is getting short and I haven't gotten through. Will they come back?" You can't be thinking about that. It's all about listening. It's all about service. It's all about trying to help them understand.

If I was going to add another component it would be to enjoy yourself. Enjoy the process. If I'm not enjoying the process, I know I'm not doing good. Listen, enjoy, be of service, and trust what occurs to you.

Take it step by step. Don't be looking at the end point. That's a bad idea because you never know where it's going to go. You never know what they are going to get. You never know what they are going to realise that's going to help them. It's a partnership. It's all a partnership. You are in it together. In a way you are not putting anything into the client or instilling anything. You are a catalyst to help them wake up to their own understanding, which is already in them, but they have forgotten. Everybody has what they need, they just forgot. Your job is to wake them up, like, "Hello, wake up, wake up". So, in a way it's not teaching. It's not coaching. It's waking. It's going around with a bell waking people up to what they already know.

It's very humbling because a lot of people get caught up in, "I know more than the client". Again, people fool themselves with thought. You just have to realise what you know. It's a game of realisation. That's what you are looking for, new thought, and new understanding to break old patterns. New understanding will break thought and raise your level of consciousness.

What happens within you if you get into trouble with a client? What do you do?

The only way I would get into trouble is if I got an attitude, was arrogant or broke rapport. That's when people react. If you are listening and there's nothing on your mind and you're in service, it's really, really hard to get into trouble because you are not arrogant, you are humble. Being in service is humble. People don't react to humble. When somebody is humble, they don't feel like a threat. When somebody is 100% trying to help, people feel that you are really on their side so you really can't get into trouble.

Is problem solving for a client the end of the story? Or do you go further?

I want them to see problems as thought, to the extent that they see that their problems are made up. What I also want them to see is that they are making up problems. So, I want them to see a deeper point than the problem they come in with.

In a way I don't really care about the problem they come in with. The problem they come in with is a metaphor for the understanding, to show them that they are making up problems. If I help them solve this problem, they'll just come in with another problem. I want them to see a broader picture, a deeper understanding of the phenomena of problems, that we make problems up and there are no such things as problems. The experience of the problem is only in a person's mind, and they made it up. When people see that point deeply, what will happen is they start making up problems and they go, "Oh I'm making up problems" and they stop. Isn't that interesting? There are no problems except in the mind of the person.

For example, if a client says his wife is critical, and they see that as a problem (irrespective if she is in fact critical) they make it into an issue. They are making it into a "you can't be this way, or this doesn't work for me". They could see this in a different way. There is always a lot of new thinking, new realisations that people can have that they will see that it's not a problem. For example, they could see that underneath the criticalness, their wife is frightened, and they have compassion.

I'm giving you examples of people who have seen that they have made something into a problem, and they didn't need to. Another example is someone could go to their wife and say, "Are you unhappy with me?" The wife could be so affected by the husband coming and saying that, that they respond, "I'm just unhappy and I'm taking it out on you". This creates a whole other conversation that's helpful.

Another client I had, realised that he didn't have to take everything seriously. So, when his wife was annoyed, he didn't take it seriously, he saw it as mood related. He didn't react to it.

So, there are deeper understandings that people can have that release them from so-called problems. They realise they can get new thought and they can see things in a different way that relieves them from the problem. But that's just a metaphor because it can be any problem they can do that with.

In a way there is no such thing as a problem. People get an expectation and define it as a problem or see something in a certain way and define it as a problem. Well you don't have to see it that way. There are so many ways of seeing things if you go to a deeper level of understanding, a deeper level of consciousness. It's not thinking about it in a different way, it's *seeing* it in a different way, *seeing* not thinking. That has everything to do with understanding and realisation, a deeper realisation, a deeper understanding. You don't have to see things the same way, "I see it this way, I see it this way, I see it this way". Well yeah you could keep seeing that way and get nowhere.

I think what you are describing could be a distinction between some "traditional" coaching styles and Three Principles coaching – the traditional styles often solve problems.

Well, yes that's nice. They get to be a problem solver and clients use the coach as a problem solver, but for example they are giving them fish rather than teaching them to fish. The idea is to teach them to fish, not give them fish. What I mean by that is that if you show them that they can go inside for their own answers, they don't need you. They become their own best friend and counsel.

Is the feeling important for you when working with clients?

Yes! It's all about the feeling. If you are insecure it's going to be difficult for you to help your client. If you don't like your client, it's going to be difficult. If you aren't present, you need some version of a positive feeling. That could be neutrality (which is actually a beautiful feeling). You can step it up and have the feeling of love. You can have the feeling of enjoying working with them. You can have the feeling of light heartedness. You can have the feeling of calm. Feeling really matters.

I check my feeling, "Where's my feeling?" For me, my Achilles' heel is that I get impatient. So, I am checking my impatience a lot, getting off my impatience, putting it aside, to go back to a feeling.

It's only professional to be in the right feeling as a Three Principles practitioner. Again, the right feeling is a secure feeling not an insecure feeling.

The feeling is everything because you want to bring the client into your feeling. You don't want to go into theirs because they are coming with insecurity. You want to bring them into security, so they relax and learn. People learn from positivity and when they relax. They listen when they are relaxed.

Could you share a story or stories of what worked well and what didn't and what are the takeaways?

Something I have learned is to find out where people are, how much they want help, otherwise you just go around and around with them and get nowhere if they don't care. They have to want help.

I've learned when I go around and around in circles it's usually because they are not into it or they are really pessimistic or negative. I have to say, "Before we can look at your depression, we have to look at your cynicism, pessimism, and hopelessness about being here".

So I've learned that when I go circular and go nowhere with clients it's because they are just not into it or the contract is wrong – I've tried to help them with something they don't want help with – and so I say, "What do you want help with pessimism, cynicism or hopelessness?" They haven't looked at it that way before. It's like a new thing and they get interested.

Chapter Six

George Pransky PhD

"Mental health lies within the consciousness of all human beings, but it is shrouded and held prisoner by our own erroneous thoughts."
Sydney Banks

What does coaching from the Three Principles or being a Three Principles coach mean to you as in the definition?

Being a Three Principles coach is in every instance improving the psychological fitness of our clients and we use their situation as a metaphor for doing that. If a coach is successful, the client's psychological functioning on a go-forward basis is better than it was before they met with you. They see it as personal to them because we are using their situation as a metaphor for teaching them about how the mind works.

What's the driver behind the way you work with clients? Your philosophy?

My philosophy is to teach understanding to the client and what enables me to do that, is the extent to which I've gained understanding for myself. So, whatever is real to me, that has had a positive influence on my psychology, is what I teach. The important thing is that I stick to that. I don't go beyond what I see for myself. I stick to what little I know. So, my philosophy is to come from that point, to an understanding of life and an understanding of how the mind works.

If there was one thing you could tell your younger self about working with clients, what would it be?

If I had to do it all over again, the one thing that stands out to me is I would absolutely do more listening and understand my clients better before I opened my mouth. When I first started, I was "too much broadcast" and "not enough receiving". I wasn't speaking in such a targeted way for the specific client I was with. In other words, I was using a shotgun rather than a rifle. If I had to do it over again, I would have been listening and more curious about the client's world and would have gotten a smaller target to talk to than I did.

How many years has it been?

I think I saw my first client in this understanding in 1978.

Do you prepare for a client session and if so, how?

Let's say I saw a client this week, I wouldn't prepare for it. For the first session I would listen. Now let's say I'm seeing them again this afternoon or next week, I don't intentionally prepare, but things will come to mind that I was curious about in what they said in our first meeting. I might have a specific idea about something to talk to them about. I'm open to any ideas I might get between the sessions, but I'm not particularly looking for new ideas.

Now in contrast when I do seminars I intentionally prepare. I try to get an avatar in my mind of who I'm talking to. I do intake with the people that are going to be in the crowd. I'm looking for a central point that I'm going to make. I get all sorts of ideas to support my point, so that's intentional on my part. I don't do that for client sessions.

The other thing about working this way is that not preparing makes me more responsive to what shows up when I meet with a person. That's why I don't want to do too much preparation. I don't want to interfere with what shows up.

Is that something that became clearer to you over the years or was it always the case?

It was always the case because I never know how the client is going to show up in each session. I've always thought it was very important to be open to however they show up, so I could see whatever movement there was between sessions.

What's your intention with a client, if any? Are you trying to get them to see anything?

I am. I'm trying to get them to see how the mind works because that will raise their level of consciousness. So, you could say that my intent is to raise their conscious state, raise their level of understanding. It's synonymous. I'm trying to raise their level of understanding on a go forward basis so it's not just an intellectual understanding, but an understanding at a deeper level, an understanding of the heart. With every client that's my intent and the vehicle for doing that is pointing to the nature of the human experience and the nature of how the mind works. My actual intent is to raise the level of understanding of every person that darkens my doorstep. That's very clearly what my intent is.

Is there a process to your client work? Components?

I'd be making it up, but I would say if you watched me work with 30 people you would see a process in there. You would see phases and stages. I would say that with every client, the first phase is for them to be comfortable meeting with me. I really want the client to be drawn into their wellbeing. I want them to feel comfortable, not self-conscious, and I really won't proceed until that happens. Even if it took me three sessions to get the person comfortable it would be time well spent. Normally it wouldn't take more than one meeting or one day at the most, but if it did, I'd be prepared to spend it because it makes so much of a difference if the person's mind is relaxed and they can take in what you are saying.

Next I would intake the client. Intake is seeing what they understand about how their mind works and the nature of life. So, I'm trying to understand what they see as they sit in that chair. What do they understand in their hearts? I'm looking for something that they don't understand that would be very leveraged for them. I'm asking them questions, doing intake, listening, and exploring their understanding of how they see things – what they make of this life, what they make of this situation – all those kinds of questions. I do that until I see something, "Oh, I see what I can teach this person, this will be so helpful to this person".

When I see that I then come to what I call a meeting of the minds, the contract stage. At this point I say to the person, "I think this would be helpful and the reason I say that is because you reported these particular problems and symptoms and this one thing would help all of those". I'll get a meeting of the minds of what they think would be a good thing to get help with. So, I want to get on the same page as the client. I want to get their buy-in into the direction I'm going.

This is where relevance comes in. During this phase I am trying to show them the relevance to what I teach to their situation. I find the higher the relevance the client sees, the better they listen.

Over the years I have seen the necessity for this contract/meeting of the minds phase more than I did 10 or 20 years ago so I've got keener ears for it. That has empowered my client work because the relevance factor is higher when people are listening better. There was a long time when I didn't really appreciate the contract phase unless it was really out of joint. If I had a mandated client or someone who didn't really seem interested in what I was teaching, I would try to get a meeting of the minds with them that this was going to be important and meaningful for them and they should learn. Other than that, I didn't concern myself with whether the client thought what I was teaching them was relevant or not. I figured they would see the relevance of it as soon as I got it across to them, but I didn't realise back then that getting them to see the relevance would make it easier for them to understand what I was talking about. It made a lot of sense to get them open and wanting that for themselves.

Then the next stage is the sharing or teaching stage; giving them input. When I have a contract with them, I will start talking about what I want them to learn and I'll use metaphors and examples, and I'll use the situation they brought as a metaphor. I have all kinds of different ways of teaching. This is when I share what I understand, what's meaningful to me.

How do you know when it's all over?

I'm looking for a change in their feeling. A change in their state you might say. That tells me they have heard something. Then I don't know whether it's a contact high or whether they actually understood something. Then I'll try to listen and see the extent to which it's a contact high and the extent to which it's something they actually understood.

Can you explain what a contact high means?

Any person, if I bring them up to La Conner, Washington, get them away from home and then put them with someone who is very warm, loving and peaceful, they are going to feel better. Each one of those things is going to make them feel better because they are not back at home dealing with the problems they deal with all the time. It's going to make them feel better that they are relaxing. So, all those things are going to make them feel better and I call that a contact high. The reason I call it a contact high is when they lose contact that goes away. So, they return back to their home and get re-involved in their life. The contact high part is going to fade away, but the understanding part isn't. So to the extent that they actually understood something for themselves that they didn't know before they came here that is relevant to their understanding of how the mind works, that's going to be a new level of understanding for them and that's theirs to keep. The contact high is kind of rented. Part of what I'm doing in my adjustments is seeing how much they have actually understood.

And how do you do that?

Everything that comes out of their mouth helps me with that. What they say and how they say it gives me a lot of information to work with. Making it part of my job to see how much understanding they gained is not something I did my whole career. Mostly in my career I said I'll give them whatever I can give them and then it's up to them. Now I'm not only taking responsibility for their learning which I mentioned in the last part of this interview, but also responsibility for how much their understanding has changed.

That process sounds like it could take a long time. Do you work with clients over periods of time?

I mostly do four day intensives or packages, unless I am doing a group, a company, or a seminar. I think of coaching as one-on-one. If I only did one session per week it would take a lot longer because they would also be losing some of the learning in between sessions. The four day intensive gives me steady consistent time with them. We have found that four days is enough for just about anybody.

You designed it that way because of the way that you saw it working?

When we started out, we saw people all day long. It wasn't even our idea. One of our clients insisted on it.

We used to spend all day with a client, and then one day one of them got sick, so we couldn't spend all day with them and we found out it worked better if we didn't spend all day with them, just a couple of times over the day. Then we would see people for two days over a weekend and then we'd see them for two and a half days. That was kind of hit and miss. Then we had them come up for longer. We didn't think people would do it because of work. We settled on four days through a process of trial and error.

What happens within you if you get into trouble with a client? What do you do?

There's only one way I get into trouble with a client and that's if my own feeling state gets in the way.

That's the only thing that I would call not doing well with clients because everything else my creative process could take care of.

How do you get over that?

One thing is I recognised it was my problem. I knew it was all in my thinking and I also knew I could feel warmly towards any client.

It always boils down to what's going on in our heads basically?

Yes.

Is problem solving for a client the end of the story? Or do you go further?

I don't solve problems. I help them to improve their functioning so they can solve their own problems. The only reason I listen to their problems at all is to get to know them and see what they have learned. That's one of the things that's very different about working from this approach according to me. It's not problem oriented. When the client comes in and says, "I hate my boss and it's really getting in my way", I wouldn't talk to him about hating his boss. I would talk to him about where our feelings come from and how they change. So, I'm always looking to teach them.

Is the feeling important for you when working with clients?

It's absolutely a crucial foundation. My feelings tell me when my thinking isn't right, that's one way it's crucial. They tell me when I am not going to be in a creative state, a responsive state, or if I am not going to be able to listen well.

The other reason feelings are important is they have a therapeutic benefit. Just a warm loving warm presence is therapeutic, it doesn't cure anything. It helps a client temporarily and puts them in a place where they can listen well.

When we had Pransky and Associates at its largest size, and every one of our consulting rooms was filled, if you looked in each room, you would have no idea what the client's diagnosis was or what their symptoms were. You wouldn't know who a business client was or who just came out of a facility because they were a lifetime depressed client. That is because all of the clients would be non-symptomatic and that's the result of the feelings of the person they were working with. So, all of our staff had such strong positive feelings that they would draw the health out of their client within 15-20 minutes and the clients would be temporarily non-symptomatic and as a result be able to listen really well. To boot, it would do something for them that they weren't always symptomatic and as mentally ill as they thought they were.

Feelings have a therapeutic benefit. They draw people in like a tuning fork. The practitioner is like a tuning fork of good will and positive feelings and the client has that same tuning fork in them, but it hasn't been used very much lately. The practitioner draws out a like feeling, a like sentiment, a like energy in the client. They can relax and listen. They are more hopeful. Everything a practitioner using this approach wants to happen is brought out by that. That's how strong the feelings influence the process.

That's what you were talking about at the beginning of your process, the wellbeing?

Exactly. People will say to us, "Am I good enough to work with other people in this understanding?" One of the things I tell them is, "one thing is important when you are with a client, and that is that they have to start feeling and being like you, not you feeling and being like them! If you are feeling and being like them, you are not ready to teach or coach! If you draw the health out of them so they start feeling more like you, that alone is therapeutic, but it's also going to put them in a position of listening well and you can teach them".

I remember the first time I worked with a cocaine client, I became more like them. I got speeded up and my mind was going a mile a minute. When I saw Linda she said, "What happened to you? You are all speeded up and restless". I thought, "Oh I just got like my client".

Now you can see how I'm not going to be able to help him such as I was so that's where the feelings matter too. You want the client to start living in your world rather than you living in theirs. In my mind, you are not ready to work with people unless that's happening.

Would you say that's rapport/connection?

Yes, I would. Building rapport and having your client get comfortable falls in the category of tone and goodwill.

If a university taught this, one of the classes would be vehicles for increasing goodwill. That would be one course you take and the whole semester would be how to enhance goodwill with clients. Believe me, I could fill up a semester on that one course in all I have learned. One of the areas of expertise that I have, and the people I develop have, is that they really know a lot about building rapport and creating goodwill with clients. No matter how difficult or transient clients are, they know how to get to that person and create a good feeling and good rapport.

Would you like to share an example?

A couple of examples. For instance, apology is a vehicle of goodwill. If I'm with a client and they get resistant, for example, they say "this isn't working for me, I haven't got any help", I'll apologise. I'll say, "I'm really sorry I'm doing my best here and I'm sorry it hasn't been more helpful, and I want it to be helpful, so I'd like to officially offer you an apology". Normally the person will say, "Oh you don't have to do that, I was just complaining George". That tells me the level is high and the rapport is better.

Getting permission is also a vehicle for increasing goodwill. If I have a corporate client and his boss wants me to talk to him about how badly he treats his employees, I know if I tell him what the boss says it will upset him and I want him in a good frame of mind. I want him to be in a good feeling. I'll use permission in order to accomplish that. I'll say, "Your boss talked to me about you. It's not going to be good news. He wants me to tell you why he sent you here. I know you're not going to like what he has to say, and probably not agree with it. It will probably upset you so I want to tell you when you feel that you're ready for that kind of unpleasant conversation. There is no hurry. We can do it tomorrow, we can do it late tomorrow, or I can do it in writing, however it would be best for you to hear the bad news".

Now, people do great with that, they prepare themselves. They actually actively prepare themselves. Most often they say, "You might as well do it now" and I'll say, "Are you sure?" You'll see them prepare themselves. There will be this pause and they'll say, "Yeah, why don't you do it just now". They do ten times better than if I just blurted it out. So very often myself and the people we teach, will see that when clients are not going to like what they are going to hear next we'd better get permission. Permission is a vehicle of goodwill.

Another thing we do with clients that builds rapport is we level the playing field and I'll lay the problem on their lap. It would look like, "I really don't know where to go from here. I've tried just about everything I can think of to get this across and it hasn't been successful. I'm going to need your help. You've got to help me here. We're going to be a team. We are going to be partners".

Could you share a story or stories of what worked well and what didn't and what are the takeaways?

What didn't work well is if I didn't get those phases right. If I didn't get the client to relax and feel comfortable and feel trusting. I think that has only happened a couple of times in these 40 years that I didn't ultimately accomplish that. When I wasn't accomplishing that, it didn't go well.

I remember I had someone who was in the mental health system for a long time and they believed in mental illness. I couldn't get them to sit in their chair, listen, and try to learn. All they wanted to talk about was how tough their life was, how mentally ill they were, and how stupid psychology was. It took quite a while for them to settle down and to consider they might have mental health in them.

That first phase took a really long time, but to my credit I hung in there and I stayed creative. At some point I said to them, "I can't help you to feel good if you have taken "feel good" off the table. If you are absolutely refusing to feel good, which you sound like you are doing, I don't see how I can help you". They said, "I'm not doing that. I'm just telling you the facts. The fact is I am mentally ill, and I've been diagnosed with chronic depression". I said, "I don't see that as fact". It took a while for them to see the possibility of benefiting from the time I was spending with them.

Also, I have had problems in the contract stage. I had a client who was a high-powered salesman. Having done intake with him I said, "Look your mind has to slow down. Your nervous system can't handle how fast your mind is going and you are all over the place". He said, "I don't want to slow down because that's the secret of my success". That was a contract issue. I had to work that out with him and get him to see it was in his best interest to slow down.

So, in any one of these phases a client situation can be difficult, but if I don't lose my bearings and I still have my creative process, my universal intelligence is going to be more powerful than their resistance.

Chapter Seven

Ken Manning PhD

"Within the soul of all human beings, there lies an innate spiritual knowledge that has the power to repair mental disturbances.... not through analyzing their thoughts, but by seeing the power of thought itself."
Sydney Banks

How do you describe the work you do with clients?

Someone whose main focus is helping people see the mechanics of how the mind works in creating perception and what the mechanics are behind the innate health we all have. I call it the design for success – welcome to the human system. It's really important for people to understand the mechanics, that would be the heart of it, I would say.

What are The Three Principles?

The Three Principles are living dynamics (forces of nature) operating invisibly behind the scenes of our moment-to-moment experiences that enable us to be consciously aware, to create with our thoughts and minds, and to have an organised, intelligent and productive life without having to manage every aspect of life every moment.

What's the driver behind the way you work with clients? Your philosophy?

Consciousness is a pure capacity that we all have. It's imbued with intelligence and the clearer and simpler we can live in our own consciousness from that intelligence the more successful and happier our life is going to be. The main thing that gets in the way of it is our reaction to our own thinking. We think we are reacting to the world not realising we are reacting to our own thinking. That's a fundamental fact about the human condition that most people don't understand. As people begin to realise that that's the way it actually works, a lot of what they are reacting to settles down.

As people start to realise these facts in real time it has a magnitude of impact beyond anything I have ever seen. Then life is good, the human system is designed to be enjoyable and intelligent. When you really know that and have faith in the system and orient yourself to living that way you can have a lot of success and a happy life. I think that's the name of the game.

If there was one thing you could tell your younger self about working with clients, what would it be?

Take your time and really learn what this paradigm has to offer, see it for yourself and find your own way to explain it. Don't worry about the way anybody else expresses it.

This is a very profound shift in understanding, if you let it be profound. You can do it at an intellectual level, but in terms of how you live in your own mind, it's a very profound shift.

Do you prepare for a client session and if so, how?

Most of the time I don't, but if I have a business client with a lot of complexity, I'll refresh myself on their complexity so that I'm up to speed on their language and issues because I tend to forget. Other than that I may look at some notes so that I can remember who I'm talking to and what we talked about, apart from that, I don't.

Do you think that comes from years of experience? Did you used to prepare?

Never did. I always trusted that once we got going I'd see what to do.

What's your intention with a client, if any? Are you trying to get them to see anything?

I want them to see that there is a natural design to the human system. It is intelligent and designed for their wellbeing and success. If they really see that and they see thought is a powerful thing that interferes with it then they will start clearing up their own thinking and living from that intelligent design.

Is there a process to your client work? Components?

I try to have an intensive four day retreat with most of my corporate clients. First I'll have preparation sessions just to get connected and align them with what we are doing. Then I'll have them come for four days and we will have follow up sessions afterwards. That's the bigger structure that I try to do with my clients.

Is there a process within sessions? Is there a structure or process you follow?

I explain to people what I want them to understand about how their minds work. I explain that I am going to go through a process to help them realise those facts so once they understand what I am trying to point to, I then give them lots of time and reflection to absorb and see if those things are really true for themselves. People then start to have lots of insights about their own mind and how they function. Then I have time with them to understand the implications. What does that mean for their life, their relationships and their work? Over the following months I'll have the same conversation with them over and over again to help them integrate that knowledge into their life.

So a four day intensive may lead to more coaching?

It's a programme that includes a four day intensive and six to twelve month coaching after that.

You don't do any prep for any of the sessions, you see what turns up and go with that?

I have a number of sessions before they come to find out what's going on in their life and orient them to the type of process that I just described.

What happens within you if you get into trouble with a client? What do you do?

I'm not sure what you mean by trouble? When I was a lot less experienced I would feel like I was in trouble, I don't have that any more. I guess I just get quiet and wait for an insight about what to do or have a dialogue with the client about what's going on in our process and why it doesn't seem to be working out, and see what they think.

What's the difference between now and when you used to feel like you were in trouble?

I'm not bothered by what happens, if it doesn't appear to be going well, it doesn't bother me. I get curious.

What's changed? It used to bother you and now it doesn't?

I don't get afraid, I don't get bothered, I don't get worried, I just get curious. I used to be in service to my practice or in service to the Three Principles. I used to have it on my mind how I was doing, I used to have it on my mind whether they were getting it or not. Those things are not on my mind any more. I'm just focused on being in service to the client. I find that when I am whole-heartedly just in service to the client I see enough of what I need to do that it flows really nicely. If there is a hiccup, I don't go to thinking about me or the Principles, I get curious about what's going on and what would be helpful.

Early on, people's resistance, or their lack of understanding or their lack of engagement would trouble me so I would get anxious or itchy about that. Now I figure this one might not work out and that's okay and I get curious to see what I can do. This happens mostly in our group trainings now. There will be someone having a hard time with our language or approach, or they may not be that interested in looking to understand themselves. They might get argumentative or challenging. We have learned to be kind and patient and find a way to help them settle down or at least get quiet and not interfere with the others. There have been a number that didn't get a lot from our group programmes. We have worked with 1000's of people in a lot of companies – 97% of them work out fine, but 3% don't.

Is problem solving for a client the end of the story? Or do you go further?

Our approach is we teach people to use their own mind to solve their own problems. We'll talk to them about their problems, but that's not the main event or focus. We go further! Of course, our clients are oriented to have us help them solve their problems, but don't realise they could be much wiser, insightful and efficient individually, and collaborative, resourceful and synergistic in their teams if they understood deeply how the mind is designed.

We tell them this is our engagement, we are here to explain how the mind works, that's what we do and that will not only solve this problem, but all of your problems because you'll see how to use your mind in a better way to solve whatever you need to in life.

Is the feeling important for you when working with clients?

Yes, of course. The mind is designed to be in a good feeling when it's working well and when it's not, it's an indication that it is not working well. People don't understand what I just said so I want them to understand that and the deeper feeling we get to be in the more they get to experience that. People want to live in a good feeling. Everybody does, so why not have it?

Easier said than done, right?

Sometimes it's not easy for me either.

If the feeling is not there when you are coaching, then what?

I try to get off the call as soon as possible. Or if I have a good relationship I tell them it's not a good time for a call.

Whether that's you being in a good feeling or the client?

Me. I will always stick with the client whatever they feel. I always want to get them in a good place. I want them to understand the importance of being in a good feeling. It doesn't mean I'm always successful.

Could you share a story or stories of what worked well and what didn't and what are the takeaways?

I had one client come once for an intensive, we knew he had a troubled background, but he was very private about it so we didn't find out too much about that. Later I found out he had some severe abuse as a child. He was part of a leadership team in a company and everybody else on the leadership team had done this individual programme. He didn't want to be left out so he decided to come.

He appeared to engage and then at the end of the fourth day as he was leaving to go to the airport, he pulled out his bible and a piece of paper with a number of quotes from the bible. He handed one to me and my business partner and said these are the passages I think you should study because I think you are missing the point. That was a very interesting experience. He never let on where he was coming from or what was going on with him until he was walking out of the door. We learned a lot from that. We learned a lot about how to prepare differently, what to ask people because we want to make sure we know what the relationship is like before they come. We do a lot more intake and discovery now before they start the programme. That was an interesting learning experience.

Generally when people come busy minded, they come anxious, they come troubled. We just connect as human beings, they feel the care, they feel the intention to be helpful. They relax, they open up, always looking in the direction of the Principles which is generic, it's not personal so it doesn't trigger a lot of personal thinking. Some people will start to see that there is a whole different way to look at themselves and they will relax and start having insights about their thinking. They usually have some blindspots about habits of thinking that they are just doing all the time that they don't see. So once they are starting to relax and have insights, if those things are getting in the way I'll point it out. Then they will back off, lighten up or slow down or stop freaking themselves out with their thinking. They start seeing a different way to live their life.

I know I am being generic, but this is what the story would be like if I was telling a story. People wake up to how their minds work. They see how powerful their thinking can be in being aligned with and in harmony with their inner, living intelligence and wisdom. They see the different results of either being in harmony with their innate mental health or not. They relax and they feel much better and very hopeful. Then they go home and they lose it all or not, or they lose some of it. We then have lots of conversations about remembering, dealing with forgetting and remembering again. They have more insights and more realisations that put more of a foundation of living in their balance and wisdom. When they get more foundation they get a different place to stand in their life relative to how they use their mind or think about things. That's the generic story.

Chapter Eight

Lori Carpenos LMFT

"Listening is when your babbling thought system takes a rest, when it stops analyzing and listens with purity of thought. Listening is hearing from the impersonal in absolute neutrality."
The Enlightened Gardener by Sydney Banks

How do you describe the work you do with clients?

The work I do with clients now is very different from how I was originally trained, which was quite some time ago. I received a licence as a Marriage and Family Therapist in 1985. Much of what I learned in graduate school did not make sense to me. Sitting through a class on diagnosing people really turned me off to the field. I thought, "What right does one human being have to label another human being?" Honestly, it felt pretty crazy to me. Then I was told upon graduation that I would have to go to the oral exam with "a bag of tricks" so that whatever case they presented me with I would have a methodology to treat that diagnosis. Can you imagine? A bag of tricks? I thought, "Are you kidding me?" But I was very shy in those days and I'd never think of questioning anyone in authority. Thankfully all fields evolve over time.

Luckily, in 1985 a good friend took me to hear Sydney Banks speak and in that very first talk, I heard that it's not up to me to make my life go the way I think it's supposed to go. In what seemed like a blink of an eye, I felt flooded with relief; a feeling I had never had before. From that moment on my life got easier and I realised this was what I had hoped the field of psychology would do for people. I never looked back, not once. I knew that I had to learn as much as I could to help my future clients. Now I tell psychology students to view their training as the history of psychology and listen deeply to what Sydney Banks realised about the human psyche.

At the time, I had no idea how to integrate what I was finding into a helping career. But then, as I recall, there was a point when Syd spoke about Three Principles; Divine Mind, Divine Consciousness and Divine Thought. I now had something I could explain to my clients that would make sense. Three Principles that explain how every human takes formless spiritual energy and brings it into the world of form. That was tangible for me. That made sense to me.

Everything I had learned before encountering the Three Principles was about trying to change already formed thought. What a huge revelation to me when I realised that we can't change something that's already formed. And that doesn't matter because thought doesn't mean anything unless we stamp meaning onto it. And furthermore that's just more thinking – thinking about already made-up thoughts.

The Principles helped me realise that it's just about seeing that we create every experience we have, through the gift of

Thought and Consciousness, in the moment. The past is over, it doesn't exist any longer except through a memory and we all know how memories change over time. Seeing that the experience of life is only pure in the moment, presented an enormous difference! That's why it's sometimes referred to as an inside-out understanding. Because all of our life experiences come through us; yes we can agree there is a person, a chair, or a tree, out there, in front of us, but everyone's experience of them is brought through their thoughts about them.

Eventually, I realised I didn't even have to talk about the Principles unless that's what made sense according to what I was hearing from my client. To me that meant I had to listen with a quiet mind.

My work as a Three Principles practitioner is about listening. Listening to the experience of the client without my own thinking in the way, without my own judgment or agenda in the way.

I listen to their world view, how they see things. It's going to be different to how I see things. It's getting inside the client's head rather than the old way of coaching or counselling which as far as I knew, was trying to put your head, full of thoughts, into the client's head. Certainly a paradigm shift from what I learned in graduate school.

I'm not trying to fix anyone because there is nothing to fix. Everyone is a perfect soul with imperfect thinking. I'm not telling them anything that they should do, I'm not giving them my experience unless it's a story that will help them see that they already have all the innate mental health they will ever need. It's just a matter of uncovering it.

A Three Principles practitioner's role is not to provide answers, it is to draw the answer out of the client. No one needs answers from someone or something outside of their own wisdom. They already have the answers, it's just covered up with a lot of problematic thinking.

Something that still amazes me to this day, all these years later, is that people's lives can transform so much, across the board, simply by gaining a deep understanding of where their experience always comes from; that such a simple understanding actually lifts a person's level of consciousness still blows me away.

What are The Three Principles?

Mind, Consciousness and Thought. I like the way Syd spoke of Divine Mind, Divine Consciousness and Divine Thought because without any one of these spiritual gifts we would not be able to experience life. Mind, the source of everything, is also the source of Consciousness and Thought. Consciousness brings whatever we think to life.The Principle of Thought gives us the power to create images, ideas, concepts; whatever you can think of, it was created by this power. We experience what we think. And Syd likened the Principle of Thought to the rudder of a ship. We can steer ourselves away from rocky shores with the gift of free will. We don't have to entertain any thought that is not in our best interest and the best interest of others. It's so simple once you see it, and then you'll continue to see more as time goes on.

The Principles are the basic building blocks of the entirety of the human experience. Finally, I had an explanation for many life mysteries i.e., why people see things differently, why it makes no sense to blame yourself or others, why the same person behaves differently at different times, why people change their minds, and on and on....

"Mind, Consciousness and Thought are the three principles that enable us to acknowledge and respond to existence. They are the basic building blocks, and it is through these three components that all psychological mysteries are unfolded."

The Missing Link - pg 21 - by Sydney Banks.

What's the driver behind the way you work with clients? Your philosophy?

I point people in the direction of their own innate health and wisdom through understanding how we all function in life. A direction within, going within, to a quiet mind, to a place where answers will come to them from a deeper wisdom, when they're not looking for them in their intellect. The client already has their own answers underneath their self-limiting beliefs. It's really a non-intellectual approach, guided by a deeper wisdom that comes through a quiet state of mind.

Sometimes I simply point out when I see a shift happen in the moment. Maybe they are pretty heated up one moment and the next they are quiet and reflective about something that was just said. If I point that out to them they can see how it works in real time.

If there was one thing you could tell your younger self about working with clients, what would it be?

I would definitely recommend finding a good mentor who has a nice feeling. I could have really, really used a good Three

Principles mentor when I was in my 20's. I was a lost soul then. For new practitioners I would suggest looking at the 3PGC* practitioner list and choosing somebody they get a good feeling for, somebody they feel rapport with. Work with them. Work with as many of them as you resonate with. I'd love to see this be a common thing for youngsters because 20 year olds are not going to their parents, and even if they did they would just get that parent's world view of things. Some will go to an older sibling or an uncle or grandparent, but to have a Three Principles mentor, somebody who is not related and has no agenda, what a gift for someone in their 20's, or any age, for that matter!

When I first began to see clients I would have told myself to rely on Mind to guide me; to know that literally no one needs to be fixed or changed in any way. People just need to be shown their own wisdom.

Do you prepare for a client session and if so, how?

I try to slow down and I get quiet in my mind, empty my mind out. There's a feeling of interest and curiosity. It's like I almost can't wait to find out what's going on in the mind of this person I'm going to meet. I really want to start with a totally blank slate and just hear what they're experiencing. Most importantly, I get into a nice feeling if I'm not already there.

What's your intention with a client, if any? Are you trying to get them to see anything?

To see how, through the power of Thought, we take formless neutral energy and create our experience through this ability to think; we create an experience for ourselves. This ability to think allows us to know creation as well as create experience. It is so powerful to see the fact of thought as opposed to what the power of Thought creates. Whatever the power of Thought creates – whether that's imagination, temporary illusion, self criticism, self-limiting beliefs, the stories we tell ourselves and believe in the moment – it's just in that moment. It's the experience of the moment which is always shifting and changing.

No experience lasts forever, they are all temporary – whether we label the experience we're having as good or bad. It's super helpful to realise that, it takes the fear factor out of our experiences. We are designed to let go of fear; in really difficult situations, people get an automatic surge of adrenaline that has them take action and then when the situation calms down they look back and can't believe they were able to take care of things in the moment rather than go into shock. It happens naturally, and proves that we can always depend on the intelligence behind life. It takes care of us!

It's also important that they realise they have innate health. They are not damaged, no matter what happened to them – nothing and no one can take away that core of innate mental wellbeing. It's still there. There are so many examples in life that prove that point whether from my own life, clients' lives, or friends' lives. We are making it all up and yet it looks like it's coming at us. It's as though there is no other way to see this event, person or circumstance until another perspective happens to come to mind and we look back and realise how different things can appear in different moments. We go up and down in levels of consciousness and changes of state of mind. We can forget that fact in the moment when something looks so real.

Is there a process to your client work? Components?

First and foremost it is listening to the client which is also described as intake – taking in the client, taking their view of life into your mind. It is understanding how they are seeing things through deep listening. I'll check in with them to make sure that what I heard was accurate, for example, "Sounds to me like you worry a lot in your life" or "Do you find you get very anxious and insecure?" Whatever I'm hearing I'll check it out with them. If they agree, I'll say, "Do you get the sense that it's possible to live without as much anxiety as you have? Or as much worry as you have?" And they might respond, "Oh no, because everybody in my family was a worry wart, so no, I think smart people worry". That's what I hear sometimes. So it's my job to explain that it's not impossible for people to have major shifts in their habits of thinking, and it happens through insight.

I give them feedback to help them realise the particular type of thinking they are doing that has gotten in their way. How buying into that line of thinking becomes a self-fulfilling prophecy – when we buy into it we make it real. We set it in motion and we act as if that's reality. If we act in that way, there is a feedback system and we are going to get life feeding us back from that level of thinking. In other words, when we take our view of things as the only view possible, we act accordingly and then get the result of that line of thinking.

For instance, if someone believes that worry is valuable and it gives them the information they need, they could worry excessively over their child and impede the child's natural growth and development. This could create insecurity in the child who now believes they are not capable of taking care of things that their peers take care of on their own, which causes validation for the parent to worry! I find it so interesting that we get what we think unless we recognise that what we think is not absolute truth, it's our personal perception of things. Knowing that fact, opens people up to greater possibility and a calmer mind.

We all have certain blind spots that are incredibly liberating to uncover. We don't have a choice in how we behave if it's the result of some thinking we're doing of which we have no awareness. It's done in innocence. I like the term, "psychological innocence". It is so important for people to see that whatever story they are caught up in, it's like "welcome to the human condition", who hasn't gotten caught up?

I had a client who told me when she notices herself thinking something ridiculous she says, "Oh no, my human is showing." What a great way to put it, since we can all get carried away with our human thinking. It's only illusory thinking that gets in the way – our own illusion of who we are and what we are capable of – self-limiting beliefs. Literally, any time we believe our negative, judgmental, critical thoughts about ourselves we are essentially blocking ideas and possibilities. Every person is part of the unlimited creative intelligence of the Universe, whether they realise that fact or not.

What happens within you if you get into trouble with a client, what do you do?

If I feel like we have lost rapport, I will adjust – it's about the feeling. I go back to a quiet mind and I look for a nice feeling so I can listen without anything on my mind. If I feel like they've gotten upset with something I said, I might say,

"What did that mean to you?" I'm going to check in and find out what that meant to them. What did they hear that upset them? Then I can show them where they misunderstood if I didn't mean it quite that way. So it's always coming back to a nice feeling of connection and deep listening that connects people. You don't even have to be in a client session for that. Anybody you are really present with, without your own personal thinking on your mind, is going to feel the connection.

I stay as grounded as I can, in my understanding of the power of Thought and Consciousness to bring thoughts to life. I don't want to get pulled into whatever trouble they got into so I just ask questions that will help me understand more about what happened in their experience and what they don't understand about how thought works.

Is problem solving for a client the end of the story? Or do you go further?

I wouldn't call it problem solving since perceived problems work themselves out when the client deepens their understanding of how reality really works. I know in the field of therapy there's this "solution-focused" approach where the client comes to get something solved, but really there's no problem that needs solving. There's understanding, first of all, that it looks like a problem because of the way they're thinking about it.

It doesn't mean that there aren't challenges in life, there are plenty of challenges. But if you look at it as an interesting challenge versus, "this is a problem and we've got to fix it", that right there is going to open up a person's ability to have a wonderful answer come to mind. There is usually more than one solution.

I think it's really helping clients see that perspective – seeing things as a question or challenge versus seeing things as a problem. When people see problems they immediately go into their intellect to try to figure them out and that's not a good way to go about it. If you ask yourself a question that you'd like a solution to or you bring it up with your partner who's involved in this question, you really want to be in a relaxed state of mind and let it come to you. It's trusting in the power of Mind to deliver wisdom. So often, answers have come to me when I least expect them – driving down the street, walking home from wherever I am, in the shower, etc.

Things have a way of working themselves out. It's one of the miracles of life to me how that works. So many things look like a problem because of how we are looking at them – that's really the key right there. I wouldn't suggest that someone look at it a different way because they would have to use their intellect to figure it out. That's what we call outside-in counselling or coaching. People will see it a new way when they've calmed down. I know that for a fact, I've seen it many times and experienced it myself.

Sometimes people will not be able to listen if their mind is on what they would call a problem. For example, when working in a housing project and a resident believes the school is treating her child poorly, and we have not yet established much rapport. In such a case, we may have to first work with the resident to help her solve her problem before her mind will be able to settle down enough to listen. That's just common sense.

Is the feeling important for you when working with clients?

Absolutely yes. It's really important to be in a nice feeling. We can't regulate the client's state of mind but we can certainly look for a nice feeling within ourselves. Whatever their experience is at the moment, I want to meet them there, but that doesn't mean that I have to drop into a lower state of mind to have rapport with them. I don't have to feel what they're feeling, I just have to understand what they're feeling. I want to be in a really nice state of mind without anything on my mind whether that's about what happened to them in the past or what the future might hold for them. It's important that I stay focused on this moment we're sharing now.

Could you share a story or stories of what worked well and what didn't and what are the takeaways?

A client once thought I was suggesting she keep her affair from her husband when I really meant that she could break it to him slowly after he understood why she was seeking attention elsewhere. If the affair was the initial focus, it would be harder to step back and see the big picture and for each to see how they contributed to this outcome.

Takeaway: Sometimes something will occur to me after a session, out of the blue, that a client may have taken something I said the wrong way. This happens as a result of the power of Mind pointing out what I need to know, so it occurs to me out of the blue, not when I'm thinking about it. If that happens, I would contact the client and make sure s/he understood what I was trying to say by asking them what they heard me say. If I told them what I meant without asking them first, I'd be putting words in their mouth – again, back to listening to the client's thinking, rather than my own thinking. Having an understanding of how that works has helped me trust in the wisdom of Mind.

What has worked out the best for me is seeing clients intensively, in a retreat atmosphere, where they can immerse themselves in the understanding of innate health and The Three Principles. I meet with them several times a day while they read or listen to Sydney Banks or other books, videos, or podcasts I recommend, from a list of Three Principles practitioners, that I think would help them gain a deeper understanding of how they work, psychologically and spiritually. This can be accomplished right from their home online together. An alternative option is from a hotel that is near my office and they meet with me in my office, which I think is even better for people to get away from their usual setting. The best way, I think, is in a get-away retreat setting. I was recently asked to offer retreats at an all-inclusive resort in the Caribbean which I'm really excited about because with everything taken care of for the participants, there doesn't leave much for them to have on their mind other than to be immersed in the present moment and a deep dive into the Three Principles.

Just speak from what you know as absolute truth – let wisdom guide you and wisdom will never steer you wrong.

*3 Principles Global Community www.3pgc.org

Chapter Nine

Joseph Bailey MA, LP

"I'm trying to help them have insight and to appreciate their insights; to help them realise they already have the answers they seek, that the answers are within and they have heard them all their life but just didn't trust them. Now they look back on their life and with hindsight can see all their previous insights. I'm just trying to help them see they have this inner guidance system that's guiding them through life. That's my intention, that's what I'm trying to help them see - that they can trust themselves. It's what I do with practitioners when I am training them - to trust themselves more."

Joseph Bailey

How do you describe the work you do with clients?

I love the word educate – it comes from the latin word *educar* which means to bring out rather than to put in. My role is to bring out that innate capacity to have: clear thinking, insight, creativity, good decision making or good judgment, to be true to oneself, and to listen to that guidance system we have built into all of us. You can call it wisdom or common sense or innate mental health. It's to help people listen to that rather than their conditioned habitual thinking of what we would call the ego, or the created self, i.e., the identified thoughts that we have and believe that's who we are.

I help my clients see that they are not who they think they are and to see that they created who they think they are. If they don't like what they have created they can recreate from a different place. The usual creation is formed from what their parents said or what they learned from their peers or through the bumps and squabbles of life – and so they learned to create a kind of protection. They can recreate their lives by awakening to what's already their destiny, their purpose or their true calling in life.

That's true for anyone, whether they are coming to me because of their vocation or they are coming to me because of a personal mental health issue. I see myself as an educator and also as a healer.

I don't really have a process other than really listening deeply to people. That's always my first step, to really listen deeply to the person because when I listen beyond my intellect, from what we would call deep listening or listening from the heart, that's where I find my guidance from within – it just springs out of listening. I see how to respond to what they need in a way that's tailor-made for them and in a language that they can hear.

This process doesn't fit well in an academic sense. When writing an academic book they are looking for a process or steps or a protocol or a prescription of how to help others.

Facilitating with the Three Principles is very organic, it's very in the moment, a very hand to mouth kind of approach.

Yesterday, I was working with a woman who was severely ill and has seen every type of specialist in the world for some major chronic diseases. She was a very gifted athlete for much of her life, playing at university and college level in several sports, in fact her whole life was sports. She was very aggressive and very competitive. She has approached her illness with that same kind of drive, intellectualising, trying to figure it out, and never giving up. She has been trying to cure herself for the last 17 years, so she is very hopeless and despairing. She came upon the Three Principles and thought that maybe this will do it.

I had to help her see how she already knew this in herself, and her sports, so she could get in the ballpark of what I was talking about. I asked her to give me examples of when she was in the zone playing golf, basketball or volleyball, and different things she likes to do. I asked her, "When you are in that zone are you thinking about what you are doing?" She said, " No", but realised afterwards, "Oh, I really was in the zone! I wasn't even thinking about what I was going to do, my hands were in the right position and I didn't even have to think about it". I explained, "That's the power of Mind, it uses the brain and all the skills. You already know how to hit a basket, and you already know how to use the golf clubs, but if you get your intellect in the way of that knowing, it can prevent you from being in the sport zone. The same applies to the natural healing zone. Work with your doctors and do what you need to do on a physical level, but you need to get your thinking out of the way of the body's natural capacity to heal itself".

I'm just starting with her. I am trying to get her frame of reference; her culture, her language, how she sees her problem and that means listening comes first. After that I don't even know, it just comes out of my mouth. I don't make it up, it just comes out. I'll ask questions, I'll tell a story, but it will spring out of that listening, spring out of the need of the client in front of me rather than some prescribed, preformed concept of what to do with every client. I don't have a programme.

What are The Three Principles?

The Three Principles are invisible spiritual powers that allow us to experience life.

Mind is the universal energy of all things, the universal intelligence of all things, not just human beings, but the entire universe is made up of an intelligent force. That's why the planets don't collide, that's how forests grow, that's how seeds turn into an oak-tree, that's how everything works. There's an intelligent force behind it. As human beings we are a part of that universal Mind and an expression of it in our form.

Universal Mind is the source of all new thought. Syd Banks called it original Thought. All original Thought comes to us via Mind. Think of Mind as the World Wide Web. What you have on your computer is all the information that you've stored there – all your habits, conditioning, personality, issues, language or culture, etc – that's all known. It's stored in the biological computer we call the brain, that is not Mind. Mind is more like the World Wide Web that has all knowledge, every library in the world, every piece of knowledge ever created and everything that's been created and everything that is yet to be created. Mind is the source of all life, of all intelligence – that's what we're plugged into. It's like that's the plug in the wall to Source. That's Mind.

With Mind, as a human being, we have the power to think. We create our unique separate reality with thinking – our unique way that we interpret whatever is happening in our surroundings. So our experience doesn't come to us from our circumstances and our surroundings, but it comes to us in the moment from our perception, which is to say our thoughts in the moment *about* our circumstances – past, present or future. It includes all of our relationships, our job, what's on the news and everything. How we experience comes from the inside-out as a function of the power of Thought which is the power to create our unique psychological experience.

The third Principle of Consciousness is that we can be aware we are doing that – it is self-awareness. When you can be aware of the thoughts you're creating, some from the past, some from habits, some from insight, you can be aware of the truth of that thought because your Consciousness is your conscience. It's your truth meter, it's your wisdom in the moment that allows you to be aware of how you are using these three powers to create your experience and the quality of the experience. Consciousness allows you to have a free will to self correct.

The Principles are like a GPS so that no matter how lost we get we can always get back on track because the GPS shows you where you are in relation to where you want to go. It gives you clear accurate positioning. It's a global positioning system. This would be a global principles system! The global principle system that allows us to navigate our ups and downs, our moods, habits, circumstances and challenges that we all go through in life. You can never know what the future is going to bring, you can never know what you'll have to deal with, but if you know that you can trust your GPS to find your way then you don't worry, you don't get so stressed, you don't take your thinking so seriously. It allows us to move through a very uncertain future with a calm knowing of certainty which is often referred to as mental health, resilience or a healthy attitude. When we are operating consciously from the Principles rather than unconsciously we are able to make those adjustments and corrections.

What's the driver behind the way you work? Your philosophy?

Philosophy is how you see life. My philosophy is that everybody is born resilient and innately healthy so I see my philosophy as one of seeing the health in the client, even when they themselves don't see it. I am working with the health within them and putting frames around that when it pops up, rather than talking about issues or problems. It doesn't mean I don't talk about problems, I don't avoid that.

Take the client example above, I had her just close her eyes and I asked her to imagine what it would feel like if she could summon the same feeling of being in the zone. And then I asked her to get in her head about her physical ailments. What would that feeling of being in the zone feel like? She got very peaceful and she smiled. When I asked her what she was experiencing she said, "I was feeling really peaceful and then this thought came up in my mind – 'oh you have tried this before – you have taken courses on self-compassion and that didn't work either', and so on". She had this whole train of frustration that came through. I explained to her that the part of her that was aware that she was having that thinking, was who we were going to be talking to. I went on to explain that she isn't those thoughts, that they are not truths and they are simply the consequence of a habit of thinking she has developed. This habitual thinking keeps interrupting her and making her feel discouraged and hopeless and inevitably her spirits sink.

I enquired as to what happens to her pain when she is in that type of feeling. She said it gets worse, that she gets a lot of pain. I asked further – "What happened in that moment when you got peaceful? What happened to your pain?" She said, "I didn't have any pain at that moment".

That's just an example of the process and my philosophy is that I think people already know this. They have been living and experiencing it their whole life but they haven't been able to identify what it is that's working and also, they have covered up a lot of the natural ability that you see in a young child. Young children know how to get over the past, they shrug it off and they are very curious. They learn very quickly because they are not afraid of being stupid, or getting it wrong or making a mistake. They have to learn and acquire all that self-judgment, criticism and self-pressure and it's that that holds back our natural resilience. It blocks the ability to self heal from problems and illness, the capacity to be creative and innovative about operating in the world; in relationships, at work and living life.

My philosophy is that I will use anything that helps the client. I don't have a preconceived programme to give them, for example, "Just learn the single paradigm* and you'll be fine", that's something I understand and I operate from. I might never mention the diagram** with some of my clients and with others I may use it to explain the outside-in and inside-out experience. I learn from every Three Principles teacher and from many other teachers. I am just a glutton for truth wherever I can find it! I'm not married to the Three Principles, even though I consider myself a Three Principles teacher, writer, coach and therapist. I'm very open to learning and seeing the common thread in all philosophies and 'ologies' rather than judging and dismissing them as not good.

If there was one thing you could tell your younger self about working with clients, what would it be?

Get this for yourself first, listen to your clients, and learn from them. They will show you how to do this. Listen to them, they will teach you how to help them. Trust your instincts, even if what arises sounds like something you have never heard before, go with it, it's usually inspiration coming in the moment. Keep growing yourself as this isn't something you arrive at and you become the expert. Your stories of failure with the Principles is the richest material to give to your clients because they are struggling, and when they see you still struggling after 38 years, they realise they don't have to do this perfectly.

I remember when I first met Sydney Banks in 1980, I was already in private practice and had worked for many years as a therapist in the addictions field. After I heard Syd and I went back to my private practice office the next week, and did what I would normally do, it didn't feel right any more. I couldn't do it anymore and I didn't know what to do. I had no language, no words, to describe what Syd had said. I couldn't even remember what he said, but I knew what he said was true. I didn't know how to apply it to counselling and coaching so I immediately signed up for a year-long internship in Florida with Roger Mills and Rick Suarez. There were five of us first including Keith Blevens, and Christine Heath, and sometimes Syd would be there.

We'd go down every couple of months and spend a week or so and I just wanted to know how do I apply this and how do I teach this? They would say, "Catch the ball before you run with it Joe!" "Get this for yourself and then you will naturally pass it on to other people". But being the clinician I was, I wanted to know what the technique was, how do I say it to them or how do I talk to them. There weren't even Principles then. We talked about Mind and Thought but it wasn't called The Three Principles. There were no books, no tapes, no videos, there was nothing! We were completely on our own. They just said live your life and as you have insights you will have something to share with your clients.

Honestly, I had no idea what I was doing! I would talk to people the best I could because in my heart I loved people, I cared about people, wanting to help them was what was driving me. Afterwards I would share something about Thought and people would look at me and say, "That was really helpful", and ask me why I had never said that before. So even though I was new and had no idea what I was doing and felt like I was stumbling through, in spite of that, I was really helping people.

People started getting well in two to three months and they were thanking me and not needing me anymore. They would be elated at the end of a session, saying they had learned so much. Previously they would leave crying or upset and that was my sign I was doing a good job – if they left crying they were getting in touch with their feelings! That was the model, you had to get in touch with all your anger, your sadness, your resentment – all of that, but they started graduating very quickly. Normally people would stay in therapy with me for at least a year, if not several years, and it involved bringing in their family and their spouse which meant I would do groups.

I learned to kind of wing it and trust my instincts early on – my clients actually taught me what was working and what wasn't. I could see that certain things would help them through witnessing their insights and I would nurture that insight more. I learned as I went. I discovered how to translate Syd's understanding of Mind in the coaching/therapy process. A lot of my clients were therapists and pretty soon they would say, " I need to learn how to do this and to start a class". So I started a supervision group with Christine Heath and as we were teaching them we would learn how to articulate what it was we were doing, because we teach best what we need to know.

Through teaching others how to do coaching/counselling, I began to see how to train people to do this and how to put some words to it. So we started a training programme and an institute with a big staff – we had over 5000 clients go through our programmes. We had addiction programmes, mental health programmes, we worked with the chronically mentally ill, we worked in schools, in corporations, in hospitals. We worked wherever people wanted to learn about the Principles.

We trained a lot of people. It was all founded on the "health of the helper" – until you catch the ball, until you get this for yourself, you really don't have anything to give anybody else.

It's your passing along, we teach who we are, rather than a concept, an idea or a philosophy.

When I worked with firefighters in an educational programme or retreat, we did a lot of small group work. We talked a lot about what it was like on a first call when you had to dig that person out of the car they were buried in, what it was like dealing with the first child death. We would talk about their world and then talk about their resiliency in dealing with that. Then we would talk about what resiliency is and how it's innate and it's natural. We coached them in a very different way than we would work with a counselling client.

My main point is that working with clients is a very creative process, "in the moment", insight by insight. I draw on all kinds of things, including the single paradigm and metaphors, my own transformational stories and stories of other people. I'm just pointing to something that's already there, but invisible.

Do you prepare for a client session and if so, how?

I guess my preparation is how I live my life, that's my preparation and I come to the session open and see what's in front of me – no judgment. Even if I just had a session with the person two days ago, I try to see them fresh. That's how I prepare: a clear mind and an open heart.

What's your intention with a client, if any? Are you trying to get them to see anything?

I'm trying to help them have insight and to appreciate their insights; to help them realise they already have the answers they seek, that the answers are within and they have heard them all their life but just didn't trust them. Now they look back on their life and with hindsight can see all their previous insights.

I want to help them see they have this inner guidance system that's guiding them through life. That's my intention, that's what I'm trying to help them see – that they can trust themselves. It's what I do with coaches when I am training them – to trust themselves more.

Is there a process to your client work? Components?

No. But if there is any sense of a process it's to listen first before you speak. Really get to know the client and their world because that will show you where the door is open. Like the 16 year old I was talking to yesterday – he was talking about sports and nature – he is an eagle scout and really into that. He moved from already making up his mind, "I'm never coming back", at the beginning of the session to, "Yes, this is really cool, I really like this, this is going to be really helpful".

At the end of the session I had built rapport and he was open, so maybe the very first stage of the process is to get rapport, a willingness and openness on their part – plus hope.

If I'm working with a (severely addicted) heroin addict, that's really different to a 16 year old kid who is just having a little difficulty in school. Working with a heroin addict, the first thing I am going to do is put him in a detox bed and get his body healed; get his brain back on line and detoxify his system before I teach him anything about the Three Principles. Treat the medical condition first – nutrition, sleep, all of that – because they are dying. I'm not going to walk in and work with them the same way I would the kid I worked with yesterday.

Meeting the client where they are at rather than coming in and teaching them about the Principles.

They may not hear about the Principles until the fourth or fifth session. They may never hear about the Principles, but I'll be teaching them about the Principles. It's like the language is the language of the soul and it speaks Spanish, French and German and adolescent lingo and hip hop!

What happens within you if you get into trouble with a client? What do you do?

Getting stuck happens all the time, that's part of the process. If I feel like I'm working harder than the client, that's a sign that I need to listen some more because if I'm pushing them, they are not drawing it out of me.

I need to get rapport, I need to listen some more, I need to find the openings. Inevitably I run into resistance, but I have a lot less resistance with the Three Principles approach, almost none in fact because I am not getting them to go back and experience all their pain. Everybody wants to be happy, everybody wants to feel good, everybody wants to feel a sense of purpose, so if that's what I'm guiding people towards there is little sense of resistance.

It boils down to listening and rapport.

Quite often I am confronted with a challenging type of client. It can show up in a variety of forms – it maybe someone who's not open or has been forced by their parents or their spouse to come into a counselling experience, they're not really all on board, they are resistant or they are so attached to their problem they don't really want to give it up or they have no hope. In these sessions I have to not relate to the person's habits, but instead I have to almost have X-ray vision and see past their habits to their essence, to that core of resilient mental health that lies within each of us.

When I see my client's health, even when it's not obvious to them or anybody else, that seems to bring it out. They can feel that you're not judging them and that you're not losing patience with them like everybody else has. They can feel that you're accepting them as they present themselves. That helps them relax and calm down. When they calm down their mind quiets and when their mind quiets, that's fertile ground for their own insight. They begin to trust you and maybe even be surprised by the insights they are having. That might even be new to them because they are so preoccupied with their personal thinking they haven't had many insights recently. When their mind starts to quiet down this little insight factory will bubble up and little insights will start to come to them.

When you have an insight it takes a lot of thinking off your mind automatically. It's a magical thing – the insight clears the mind of extraneous, unnecessary, irrational thinking. Erroneous thoughts begin to fall away and when a person feels that, it lightens their burden and they naturally experience a feeling of hope. Hope allows the mind to open up and then they can hear you when you're teaching them about the Principles. They can begin to listen. But until they have an open mind it's like pouring water into a cup that has a lid on it, it just spills over and doesn't penetrate.

You could call it getting rapport with the client. For me it's seeing past their habits, which you would call pathology if you were a clinical psychologist. It's seeing beyond their habits to the essence of who they are at their core. That is what you talk to – the health in the client – and the client experiences that as being non-judgmental, accepting them, seeing who they maybe don't even see themselves as. When another person sees their beauty, their essence, it wakes them up to the possibility that maybe I can be okay, maybe I can be happy, maybe I can find peace of mind.

So again it's a very organic process, there is no set of guidelines or set rules. Each person is different so the facilitating process is very "in the moment" creative. I never know what I'm going to say. I have to get really empty when I go into the session and clear my mind of all the things I may have already created about the client and see him fresh. My job is to keep clearing my screen of all the junk. I want a fresh screen. My connection to universal Mind connects to their universal Mind and that's where transformation happens.

Is problem solving for a client the end of the story? Or do you go further?

Once people get an understanding of how they work psychologically to create experience and their life, problem solving becomes an outcome rather than a focus. Many times the presenting problem they arrive with will be gone, just by realising the problem isn't what they are worrying about – it's the fact that they are worrying about it that's the problem. So it kind of shifts from being a problem.

It doesn't mean I don't talk about the problem with them, but my goal is to help them see it from a higher understanding rather than me coming up with suggestions. It doesn't mean I wouldn't ever suggest anything, it may come to me – "It sounds like now that you feel more secure about money, it might be a good idea to sit down with someone and make a budget?" Or if it's a health issue, "You might want to see what feels good to your body, you might want to join a gym or do yoga or whatever", but I won't prescribe anything specifically.

I ask, "What are you drawn to? What do you need?" The answers might be "I really need to lose weight" or "I really need to start dating" or "I keep wanting a mate, but I don't ever go on a date". People solve their own problems once they understand how their thinking works and how insight works – it guides them to the next step and the next step. I teach them how problems are solved rather than how to solve problems.

Is the feeling important for you when working with clients?

It's not like a particular feeling is important but really caring about another person is super important in creating the rapport. So the feeling that I'm coming from has to come from within, I can't put it on like a shirt, it has to be real, it has to be genuine. So again, we are coming back to the point that the best way to prepare for this is to live *your* life the best you can. The way you live your life allows you to pass it on to other people. The more you are in alignment with how life actually works – The Principles – the happier you are; the luckier you are, the smarter you are about money and about cleaning your house.

Everything changes once you get a deeper understanding. People are attracted to the feeling you are speaking from, they sense your calm, your certainty, your ability to listen – they sense your genuine interest in them. They are all feelings that come from an understanding. The feeling is like seeing the written lyrics of a song versus watching it performed. The performance is the instrument, words are just words on a page until they are sung or they are played.

Could you share a story or stories of what worked well and what didn't. What are the takeaways for you?

Clients always want to hear about how screwed up you are, they love to hear that and people love to hear stories of hope like the woman I saw yesterday who had chronic illness. I had just seen another person the day before who had 20 years of chronic Lyme disease and had tried every form of homeopathy etc, so a very similar but different illness, and in the midst of the session she had a transformation. She was wound up tightly in the first session and she hardly let me speak. She interrupted a lot, "Oh that reminds me of this ... and when that happened to me ... and that happened to me ... but I've tried homeopathy and every time I tried it ..", and on and on. She couldn't be quiet so I thought the next session was going to be interesting.

The second session with her was the following day because she was so urgent. She said, "I have to get this *now*, the Three Principles are going to save me, I know they are". That made her desperate. I said to her, "Stop for a moment and look at yourself on Zoom and what do you see?" She said, "Oh my god, my forehead is all wrinkled!" I explained that there are three rules of thumb on how to get something out of these sessions. "Don't worry about how you are doing, you're going to be fine. Don't intellectualise about what you see. You see that little crease, it's an "I", it stands for intellectualising. The third thing is to just enjoy the sessions, that will help you to relax and you'll be more at the bus stop where insight happens".

Something hit her in that conversation and she smiled – the wrinkle disappeared. She said, "Oh my god I think I'm getting it!" and she started sobbing with gratitude and relief. I asked for permission to record the session so that she could see it later in case she forgot. It was a one-in-a-hundred session, an amazing transformation on the second session.

This became a story of hope for a woman I saw the following day. I told her about it and that gave her hope. It's a leap-frogging kind of thing. It's always different; it's never the same. It's a very creative, innovative process not a formula, or prescription, but more of a description of how the process works and then your creativity as a coach.

I love seeing how the Three Principles are going out in infinite ways – I have a lot of musicians as clients who are writing songs about it, clients who are athletes teaching other athletes about the power of the mind. So the ways that we do this are infinite and the tool is you and your creative intelligence. That's the power of the inside-out understanding.

I just want to check in on your takeaways as a professional – about what worked and what didn't?

I see that the things that don't work are like pointing sticks to what doesn't work and pointing me in a different direction, so listening to what doesn't work is really helpful in my practice and it's also helpful in life. Certain things you do are not going to work, but – if you pay attention and listen to that, and learn from it, you will keep evolving – the same thing applies to being a practitioner. That's how I had to learn, through my mistakes and my successes and it was just like following the breadcrumbs; it's like a tracker in the wilderness. If you are a tracker there are no arrows and signs, but there are leaves pressed into the ground. By the shape of the imprints you can see which animal passed, the direction they were moving in and how long ago it was and if they were running or walking. You can learn a lot from one little footprint, that will kind of give you a sense of how to keep following that and it's kind of like that with the client process: you keep looking for signals and signs that are subtle and you follow them like a tracker.

* single paradigm is an articulation of how we psychologically experience based on The Three Principles, and created by Keith Blevens and Valda Monroe www.threeprinciplesparadigm.com

** diagram – a visual created by Keith Blevens and Valda Monroe to support their articulation

Chapter Ten

Christine Heath LMFT, MAC

"When the answers are complicated, it is the intellect. When the answers are simple, it is the Spirit."
Sydney Banks

What are The Three Principles?

It is very difficult to write about the Three Principles because it becomes something intellectual and makes it hard to see how they work because we engage our intellect, but here is a shot at explaining the formless nature of life.

Mind, Thought, and Consciousness are the three fundamental spiritual Principles behind the creation and experience of reality. These Three Principles allow us to recognise and react to what is happening around us. They are the explanation of how we understand each other and our world. The Three Principles explain the psychological and personal reality of everyone, no exceptions. However, every person has a unique experience of life. The Principles explain every experience that every person has, all the time. They do not work differently from person to person and moment to moment, but they create unique and separate realities within each one of us.

People sometimes try to separate the Three Principles and talk about them individually, but they truly are one thing that works in different ways. Mind, the energy of all things, breaks down into Thought and Consciousness. It has intelligence that we refer to as wisdom. This internal knowing helps us walk through life with common sense and harmony. As this energy flows through us, it generates experiences and perceptions and allows us to share a reality with others. Thought is the ability to be thinking and use information to live our lives and Consciousness is the ability to be aware of everything – our spiritual essence, the content of thinking, and the outside world. Consciousness brings our thoughts to life and creates our psychological experience.

These simple but profound Principles will someday be responsible for a great awakening in humanity. As more and more people understand and see how the Three Principles work, they will begin to live from healthier, more loving and productive states of mind. From this vantage point anyone can see how to solve their problems and together we can then see how to solve the problems of the world. The Principles are the hope for humanity.

How do you describe the work you do with clients?

I really want people to be happy, calm and secure. That's the goal. If you are feeling better and your life is going better, and you know how to maintain this, that's great for me. When people start to see how the Principles of Mind, Thought, and Consciousness work in them, they create an entirely new reality and everything changes. Helping others is more like mentoring than being an expert and teaching something. It is helping people to see what they already know. It's pointing out the health and wisdom they have and helping them to see how their own thinking is creating the obstacles in their lives.

My way of working with clients is different from what people might expect. I am not focused on problem solving or practising techniques, fixing personality flaws or helping people to figure things out. I am just helping people awaken to what they already know and to live in a state of mind which will provide them with the direction they are seeking.

My job is to listen and draw out the health in people and help them to see what they already know about living in mental wellbeing. I do this by sharing what I understand about the Principles and how they work in everyone. I use stories to illustrate how thought can trick us into living lives that are stressful and unfulfilling. I also share my own stories of how I awaken to this daily and how others have transformed themselves and their lives.

What's the driver behind the way you work with clients? Your philosophy?

It's just being myself and helping other people to see that they're not different from me and we all work the same way. If I can be happy, they can be happy. I'm not the teacher and they are not the student. I think this is a way of connecting with people; we are just two human beings having a conversation about what I was lucky enough to stumble into. I generally find that this does a great deal to create a good connection with people.

The coaching/therapy/counselling role, from my perspective, is to really help people see what they already know; to help them demystify life and learn to live in love more of the time. In doing this, I am helping people see how they are already in a state of mental wellbeing and how the Principles work. This resilience is already in people and they don't have to do anything to get it. There is nothing wrong with them. They are not stuck.

I had a guy come to me last night who said, "Chris, everybody is stressed out!" and I let him know that I was not stressed out. His response was, "Everybody else is except you!" I said, "Maybe, but that's what I could teach you, how to live like me". He said he didn't believe in that, so I just smiled and let it go. We moved onto discussing his son who was experiencing lots of trouble at school. By the end of the session, he was smiling and said, "I don't trust many people, it's so nice to meet you". I just went back to being on an equal basis with him rather than trying to help him see that if he had less stress, his son would probably be reacting differently.

I trust that if people find that state of mental wellbeing in themselves, that will do the job for them. I'm not trying to get people to see things, and when I sometimes attempt that, I'm not very successful! I am trying to help people see that they already have what they need and it's just a question of looking in another direction rather than intellectually trying to understand things. I call that the "information application" mode where we take information and try to apply it in our life. I'm trying to get people out of that mode and to just see that everything they need is within them. I know that if they really just settle down and look in that direction, they will automatically calm down.

Mental wellbeing is like this safe, beautiful space that's inside of us. When we are processing things with thought, we're just taking the gift of Thought and doing something with it, but that's not where mental wellbeing comes from. We are taught to memorise, analyse, figure things out, and then apply what we learn to our lives. People fall into that mode very easily. But, mental wellbeing comes BEFORE the ability to process anything.

If there was one thing you could tell your younger self about working with clients, what would it be?

To be very gentle and very patient and not have expectations about how people live their lives or how people teach the Principles. In the early days, there weren't many of us and I felt like I'd been given this great secret and it was my job to get it out into the world. That created insecurity because I was like, "Oh my gosh, I have to have the perfect life and everybody I teach has got to take this out into the world and, I've got to be a better teacher, and if I'm not a better teacher they're not going to take it out into the world!"

I would put a lot less stress on myself and I didn't really trust my wisdom. At the time, I just couldn't see to do that. All I could see was that this was the cure to mental illness and stress and I could screw it up at any opportunity.

When I first learned this, there were no books, no videotapes, and there weren't even articulated Principles. All I could say was, "I went to this training where they had discovered how to be healthy and that it doesn't matter what happened to you", and I would just talk from that feeling. I had 60 clients a week, mostly groups I ran, so I would just share whatever insight I had that week. I shared what I was seeing day to day. As I shared what I saw, my clients started to pick up the feeling and they started to have their own insights.

I recorded a video with them to talk about what it was like being with me before and after and one of them said it was like I went into lightspeed. They said they didn't know what was going on with me, but they followed because they could feel there was something there, something for them. Again, at the time I remember saying, "Look, I went to a two day talk on this so this is my best shot and this is what I saw". That was the best I could see to do.

At the time, I had one Sydney Banks tape entitled, "Seminar on Mental Health", and I listened to that tape every night. I would go into work and trust that what would come through me was what was supposed to come. I saw that the wisdom was inside of me and all I needed to do was talk from that feeling about what I could see for myself. That was still much more than any of my clients had ever heard. I think trusting that feeling and talking from that feeling was my bootcamp.

The feeling is in the experience. As soon as you try to talk about the Principles as concepts, or try to "teach" the Principles, you are lost because none of us really can put this into words. All we can do is talk about the living of it and see in the moment how it works.

When I first started learning about this, Joe Bailey and I were the only people in our area that were into this work. Everyday, at the end of the day, we'd call each other and talk about how this happened, that happened, and what about this! We were in this unbelievable feeling even though we had no idea what we were doing. I see this as a clue now, that when I start thinking I know what I'm doing, then I'm not present. I'm not coming from that deep feeling of life, but instead coming from memory.

Do you prepare for a client session and if so, how?

I get myself in the best state of mind I can, clear my mind of whatever personal things I'm thinking about, and sit down and get into a feeling. Hopefully I'll be in the feeling already, but not always. Sometimes, the more information I have ahead of time about the individual, the less connected I feel. Just that little bit of thought can change things. I think that when people are insecure about what they are going to say, they go to preparation mode.

When I'm going to lead a group or a weekend event, I will have a topic and think through how I can make this understanding relevant to the listeners. For example, I'll find two or three points I want to make so I stay focused for the hour without losing my way. But usually for one to one sessions, my preparation is to let go of the last session so that I see them fresh and new every time I talk to them. Otherwise, I am in the past with them and am seeing them as they were in the last session.

Sometimes people get irritated with that because they think I'm not listening to them. I tell them I listen, but I try to forget the details. I explain that if I have our last meeting on my mind, I'd see them the way they were last week, and if they changed in between, I won't be current with them! It doesn't really matter where they were last week, it matters where they are now.

As a therapist, before learning the Principles, I couldn't understand why they had this therapy called Strategic Family Therapy where they would plan everything out before the session. I remember asking my teacher, "If the client changed in between sessions, how would I know what the next session should be like?" The teacher felt that I would know how they were going to react so I could plan based on what we know about human nature. At the time, I felt I wasn't smart enough to do that! The issue with that is, if you are planning your next session based on the last one, you are assuming the person hasn't had an insight and changed. If they have had an insight, you would be way behind the game. You would be talking to the person you talked with last time, but a new person would be talking to you!

What's your intention with a client, if any? Are you trying to get them to see anything?

My intention with a client is for them to feel better and understand that the world doesn't cause their stress. I want them to be able to see for themselves that firstly, their thinking can trick them and make it appear like the outside world is to blame for their experience. And secondly, that love and wisdom come from inside of them all the time. If they see those two things, the rest of their life is a piece of cake.

Helping people to "see" versus intellectually understand requires awakening versus information application. Many people try to intellectually share "The Principles", which, in my mind, does not facilitate a shift into a deeper state of consciousness. People tend to try to appease the intellectual appetite by applying this understanding. This is backwards, as when people listen without trying to figure it out, and when the teacher is coming from a deeper feeling, something happens and there is a shift in the person that has nothing to do with the words or the intellect. This is what is called a "realisation". This shift brings forth a beautiful feeling and then the understanding starts to flow. Insights come to people about their lives, the way their thinking tricks them, and how they can change without effort.

The thing I've learned about people is that I have no idea what they should do, and when I think I know what they should do, I am totally out to lunch! They know what they should do and I have to trust that. Sometimes that's hard for me because I think I know better! There have been times when I've talked to people and I didn't understand why they chose to go to a more traditional lecture or class while in therapy with me. Later, they came back to me and said, "Oh Chris, they are saying the same thing you're saying, we got so much out of it". Then I realised they were hearing what they needed to hear from within themselves. I just have to trust they know what they are doing.

Is there a process to your client work? Components?

Go by the seat of your pants! (laughs)

I check in with them to see how they are doing: did anything change, are they seeing anything differently? I go back to listening. I really want them to tell me what's going on. As they are talking to me, I can tell whether or not they are still caught up in the content of their problems, for example, by telling me who said what to whom. If they are starting to say things like, "I don't know what's happening, but I feel better", that helps me see they are going in the right direction, even though there is nothing really clicking with them yet. They're not buying into it, they're not looking for it, they're just like, "Oh I feel better but I have no idea why".

That's helpful and makes me look good as a helper, but it's not really deep enough for the client because they won't be able to maintain that feeling. So seeing that I can be just like any other drug is kind of a new insight for me. I have always recognised that when people are with me, they get into a nice feeling. The idea is that when they leave, they maintain that feeling, but there are times when people still struggle.

I realised I need to be more explicit about them deepening their understanding if they want more permanent change. I encourage them to do things like read Sydney Banks' books, watch his videos, and be open to hearing something different. Otherwise it's not going to be enough for them to just come and see me. I tell them, "You'll get into a better state of mind, things will change in your life, but it won't be enough for you to maintain it. You have to see what I am pointing to, I can't fix you".

Many professionals are coming from a more intellectual space. People hang out with them and they get a better feeling because the coach/therapist has a nice feeling. Then when they go out into the world, they start searching again, they start looking intellectually for something to make them feel good. It's as if they are thinking "I've tried the Three Principles, now what else is out there?" So they haven't seen that it's inside them.

I do a check-in, updating, "Where are you today, what's happened?" I'm listening for where they are and from that point on I'll go to whatever comes to mind. I usually try to encourage them to listen to audios, podcasts, or read books so that there is something in between sessions. Again it depends on how distraught the person is feeling. If they are very distraught, I might tell them to schedule more frequent sessions because one of the things I am listening for is how long the feeling lasted for them, how long did they go until they started getting caught up in their intellect again. If they don't maintain a positive state of mind for a week, then I'll say let's meet twice a week. If that doesn't do it, I'll maybe do an intensive with them.

What happens within you if you get into trouble with a client? What do you do?

I get quiet. I'm listening again to see how I can hear what the person is saying to me. If I'm not in the right feeling, I've got to clear my mind and calm down, then wait for the feeling and my wisdom to come back in and right the ship, in a sense.

It may be that sometimes I use stories or say something which inadvertently triggers another human being. When this happens, I'll say, "Wait a minute, let's talk about this because I had no idea that was something that would make you feel insecure... isn't it interesting that you thought about it that way?" Usually I take responsibility for it and I become humble and do whatever it takes to get the feeling back. Sometimes it's standing on my head, cracking a joke, taking a drink of water, or saying "Let me just reset a minute here, I got a little reactive to you there". I get very present in the moment.

When I first started out, that would happen to me and I'd be like "Oh my god! What am I going to do, I'm so out to lunch?!" Now I don't get so freaked out about bringing it back to the present, bringing it back to a feeling. I'm not nearly as judgmental about myself as I used to be. I now don't think I have to be perfect and I see that produced a lot of insecurity in the past. Now I understand that the more I'm able to be myself, the more helpful I can be.

I try not to personalise, that's the other thing. When I take something personally, and feel my emotional reaction, I calm myself and listen to get clear about what is off... me or the client? As soon as I see what is off, my wisdom guides me to get the feeling back and reconnect with the client.

Is problem solving for a client the end of the story? Or do you go further?

I almost never problem solve with a client. That's almost never on the table. If I'm problem solving with them and trying to give them good ideas about what to do, I am just giving them ideas about what I would do and that has nothing to do with what they should do. I always tell people that I have no idea what they should do, but I do know that if they get into a really beautiful feeling or quiet down, their wisdom will come to them and they will know what to do.

So I don't do problem solving or I do as little of it as possible. Sometimes people try to get me to tell them what to do so I suggest doing this or that. Then they tell me they don't want to do this or that, and I find myself saying, "See what I mean?!"

The other thing I know about people is that the state of mind they are in is what's creating the problem they want solved. So if you solve a problem one week, they will come with another problem the next. If their state of mind doesn't change, they are not going to stop having problems. So what I tell people is, "You're not here to solve your problems, you're here to learn how to live in a healthier state of mind and then you'll be able to solve your own problems. I could tell you what to do, but that's ridiculous, there's not one answer for everybody, there's not a book that says if this happens in life, do this. Life isn't like that, everybody is different. All the people you have problems with are different, there are too many variables, but you can see what to do. You have those answers within you".

Is the feeling important for you when working with clients?

The feeling to me is really being in a state of mental wellbeing so that the life force is coming through you and not to you. You are part of that, you feel alive, you feel awake, you feel a sense of knowing. It comes in different forms, but it's this sense of knowing that you're okay, that what you're doing is okay and that you are going in the right direction. It's a deeper feeling and it is difficult to talk about because if you haven't experienced it, you can't get it intellectually.

In fact, I remember when I first learned the Principles I had a shift that was unbelievable and people thought I had either joined a cult, was on drugs, or I had met a man! They were the only things that other human beings had seen in one another that would change them that much. These were my therapist friends, and nobody had ever seen a person transform that much, that quickly. I had never seen anybody transform that much! I remember all of a sudden I had this incredible feeling inside me, it was something I knew was bigger than Christine

Heath. I could feel there was something coming through me, that I was a part of something bigger and that was the source of my good feeling.

That feeling! I remember I had butterflies in my stomach for three days. I couldn't sleep, I couldn't stop smiling, my cheeks hurt because I hadn't smiled so much in so long. I was just totally different. About a month went by and I was going for a three week training and I could feel I was starting to get a little insecure about taking three weeks off and immersing myself in this. I had never taken more than five days off in my life, let alone three weeks. But, I had such a strong feeling about it, I was just going to do it.

At the training, they started talking about this feeling and I thought, "Are they talking about that feeling I had?" Like okay, I don't have it that strongly any more, so what's the deal here, what are they talking about? Something hit me that there was something deeper, a deeper feeling, and that I needed to slow down in order to see.

After about two weeks, I felt so tired I had to call up and say I couldn't come in. I got so tired I literally couldn't get out of bed. So I stayed in bed all weekend, watched tv, hung out by the beach, and basically did nothing at all. When I got up the next Monday, I had a deeper, quieter, secure feeling and I was like, oh, that's what they are talking about.

I am still learning now, aware of when it comes through me, but seeing I can't do anything to make it happen. Just trusting it and going with it when it comes through, but not thinking about it ahead of time. We've all experienced it, we've just not identified it. So you can't make it happen, you just have to be open to it happening and turn yourself in the direction and be patient.

The feeling is obviously very important to you when you are working with clients even though you can't make it happen?

It's the medium I do client work in, it's the goal of working with clients and it's the method, it's everything. It's all about the feeling for me, it's the understanding that comes with that, that will help people do what they need to do.

What happens if there doesn't happen to be a feeling in the session? Has that ever happened to you?

Oh yes. All I can do is sit there and keep directing myself back inside. I've had people get up in the middle of sessions and try to duke it out with each other. I've had lots of things happen that really wouldn't be coming from a calm, nice feeling, but that's the direction I'm going and I do what I need to do to get everyone back on track. Sometimes I have to sit there and listen to problems. I do whatever it takes for the person to settle down. I usually don't care about what they are talking about, but as I'm listening, I'm listening for where their health is so even if their health comes out for a second, I'm like okay, pay attention to that. Look at that, that's inside of you

Could you share a story or stories on what worked well and what didn't and what are the takeaways for you?

A woman I knew had been badly physically abused by her husband and I was sharing a story with her about how another woman was coming in to see me because her husband was having an affair, but the husband wouldn't come too. She had been reading Second Chance by Sydney Banks. As he was leaving her to go to Washington DC to live with this other woman he was having an affair with, she put Second Chance in his hand luggage. He read it on the way to Washington DC, called her up when he got there and said he was ending the relationship and coming home.

I told her that story and she said, "I'm supposed to get back together with this jerk?" He was dangerous and he beat her. I said, "Oh no, that's not the point of the story. The point is that this woman was really focused on sharing a good feeling with her husband, she wanted something nicer for him, and she just stayed with that and didn't really care if he was going to leave her or not.". She said, "Well it sounds to me like I should just forget about what he did to me". I replied, "This is the deal: if you are walking around with him in your head, he's still controlling you. You are the person who has the ability to change that, but you have to see this deeper for yourself and whatever the outcome is, it will be perfect for you. I don't know if you should stay with him or leave him. If you ask me personally, I would tell you, 'Man I'd leave him in a heartbeat', but I'm not you so it doesn't matter what I would do, it matters what you would do".

Sometimes I use a story that I think is hopeful, but they hear something that they think means they have to do something they don't really have a good feeling about. I've gotten better at sharing stories and helping people see the relevance to them. There are stories that I usually tell about myself, but, I've noticed it's the things I say off the cuff that really impact people. The point of telling a story to someone is to quiet them down, not to get them thinking. So if they have a bad reaction to the story I know they haven't quieted down, they are still in their head about it.

At any time, people can hear things in a way that they were not intended to be heard and, for me, that's an indication of how much they are still in their head. They're listening to their own commentary in their head about what I'm saying rather than listening for their own insight. That tells me I've got to go back and talk about listening with them, about how to listen with nothing on your mind because most people can't listen like that. Most people are listening and thinking at the same time, trying to apply what you are saying, listening to understand, or to agree or disagree. All that thinking is where their trouble is, so I am then taking them back to listening – listening with a quiet mind.

I live in Hawaii so I might say something about going to the beach and listening to the waves coming in. As people listen they feel calmer and feel more relaxed. Actually they have done studies of people who are depressed who go to the ocean and listen to the waves and they do feel better, their depression decreases. That's not because of the ocean; I live on an island and if that were true there would be no depression here but there definitely is! It's that they are present and they are listening. If they are getting reactive to me, I know they are not listening in that way and I have to go back, reset my state of mind and help them quiet down.

The beautiful feeling got me first, I guess that's why it's still my thing. I remember that listening to Roger Mills felt like stroking velvet; it felt like he was gently soothing my soul and I thought it was about him at first, but realised that it was actually me! This feeling was the thing that got me in the first place and it still does today 40 years later.

Chapter Eleven

William F Pettit Jr MD

"All human psyches are rooted in universal truth and no person's psyche is better than any other's. Only to the degree of the individual's psychological and spiritual understanding does it appear to vary."
The Missing Link by Sydney Banks

How do you describe the work you do with clients?

The first word that comes to me is "joyful". In my heart I know that what everyone I encounter seeks is an internal silence where they can easily experience their essence as a loving, divine, intelligent, conscious and creative energy living in the world of form, but of the world of spirit (formlessness).

It is as if each person I encounter has an incredible Present in the depths of their consciousness and I get to be with them and facilitate their unwrapping of it. What could be more joyful than that?

The word collaboration comes from the Latin words to "work with someone" and implies participation and contribution of both parties. In that respect I find the word collaboration inviting. However, to me even the word "work" in this manner seems inadequate if not inappropriate. "Why so?" you might ask.

The definition of the word, "work" includes the words, exertion, effort, labour and toil. I find that when my experience of my encounter with another is any of these, it is a signal for me to stop and allow my own personal use of Mind to quiet down and to listen.

Rather, I find the collaborative process of sharing the Universal Principles of Mind, Consciousness and Thought as insight-based leap frog where the shared insight of one participant facilitates the realisation of insight in the other.

Another way that I might describe sharing the Principles is that of a guide or mentor who is presently more acquainted, knowledgeable and understanding of a system than his mentee or student. A good mentor or guide can facilitate another to awaken to a greater understanding of the system in question. This is true of a forest ranger and likewise of a sharer of universal Principles.

Thus a guide, sharer, facilitator, mentor and leapfrog associate are all appropriate descriptors of my role with those who seek my assistance.

What are The Three Principles?

From the beginning of man's earthly journey, there has been a desire and quest to understand the source and nature of creation and of life. This "experience of mystery" has engendered both science and religion in a search for the answers.

In August of 1973 an intelligent, kind, hardworking man named Syd Banks sought to have a gentler experience with his wife who he dearly loved. In the process of his efforts in this regard he had a powerful experience which culminated in his having a powerful sight into the mysteries sought by man for thousands of years. See www.sydbanks.com.

The Three Universal Principles of Mind, Consciousness and Thought are the metaphor that he uncovered as a means to point to and share the spiritual Truth that he experienced.

What's the driver behind the way you work with clients? Your philosophy?

Taking the definition of "driver" as a part that transmits force or motion, then love and understanding are the dual drivers.

If one sees "philosophy" from its Greek roots, "the love of wisdom/truth" then the realisation that all that exists, formless or in form, is the same divine energy in a different disguise, would be the theology behind the way I mentor.

If there was one thing you could tell your younger self about working with clients, what would it be?

The first thing I would tell myself as a beginning student and sharer of the Three Principles would be "the journey of understanding the nature of these Principles is incremental and endless".

The second thing would be encouragement – to be gentle with myself, grateful for each insight and to enjoy the journey.

Do you prepare for a client session and if so, how?

I do my best to come to each session rested and present, with an open mind and loving heart.

What's your intention with a client, if any? Are you trying to get them to see anything?

I'm doing my best to facilitate in my "mentee/student" incremental insights into the spiritual nature of the Three Principles. Wisdom and experience informs me that this is a reliable route to happiness, contentment, love and understanding.

So that's my goal – to assist people to live in happiness and contentment regardless of past painful experiences, present challenging circumstances and future uncertainty. This can often generate questions such as "What about productivity, what about creativity?" I would respond to those inquiries by saying, "It is my personal and professional experience that when people are happy and content, they have all of their resources available to create and be productive and they are naturally motivated to do 'the next right thing'."

Is there a process to your client work? Components?

Is there a process/components to my sharing, facilitating, mentoring?

Process: a systematic series of actions taking place in a definite manner.

Component: an element.

I would say that the first step/element is establishing rapport/trust.

The second is for the student/mentee/client to share with me what they hope to gain from our meetings, what efforts they have made thus far, and what they feel they have accomplished towards their goal. The deep listening you spoke of is important in this part of the journey.

The third is for me to share what I have to contribute that will facilitate them meeting their goal.

The fourth is to establish some agreement/contract on how we will proceed.

What happens within you if you get into trouble with a client? What do you do?

Trouble: synonyms include among many others, difficulty, danger, dilemma, disturbance, predicament, commotion, discontent, concern. "Trouble" then can arrive in many forms, but all seem to point to an awareness that there is a glitch in the mentoring, facilitating process.

What do I do when I become aware that this is the case? My first step is to become as quiet and present as possible, and listen both within me and to my mentee.

From listening in the state of presence and caring, we will see the source of the "trouble" and will be guided to see what to do next.

Is problem solving for a client the end of the story? Or do you go further?

Problem is defined as "any matter involving doubt, uncertainty or difficulty". From my perspective every "problem" that people present with is life perceived through insufficient understanding of the Three Principles at the source of life and experience. When this understanding is experienced sufficiently, the presenting "problem" has been resolved. People often see the value in continuing the journey. I am glad to facilitate that journey of insight based understanding for as long as they find it helpful.

Is the feeling important for you when working with clients?

Important: of great significance or consequence

To me, when "mentoring" by sharing the Principles, the feeling or rapport between us and the feeling of unconditional love on my part is vital to the process and collaborative journey.

Could you share a story or stories of what worked well and what didn't and what are the takeaways for you.

Since being a student and sharer of the Three Universal Principles since April 1983, I have witnessed literally thousands of people who had been labelled with multiple psychiatric diagnoses find a life permeated with love, lightheartedness, wisdom, productivity, creativity and vitality that they had believed impossible.

What has worked for me has been:

1. Incrementally finding an increasing ability to live in a space of love on a daily basis despite perceptions of past, present or future challenges.
2. To show up to each human being rested and present.
3. To share from what I KNOW and experience to be true.
4. To give the best I have in both listening and sharing WITHOUT ego investment in the outcome.

5. From the beginning, to encourage my mentee/client to "sample" the source materials of Sydney Banks, six short books and three sets of videos available on www.sydbanks.com and to utilise them as they are guided to do so.

What hasn't worked is:

1. Not taking care of myself physically, mentally or spiritually.
2. Sharing from what I think I SHOULD know but what I have NOT seen for myself.
3. Falling out of love and into judgment of myself or the person I am mentoring.
4. Becoming ego invested in the outcome of my mentoring.
5. Trying to do it alone without utilising the source material from the man who had the original insights into the Principles I am attempting to point to.

Chapter Twelve

Mark Howard PhD

"It's just love and understanding."
Sydney Banks

What are The Three Principles?

The Three Principles of Mind, Thought and Consciousness are a way to understand the true nature of us as living human beings as well as understanding where our moment-to-moment experience of life gets created.

The Principle of Mind points us to the fact that we are part of a spiritual energy that contains an intelligence that was there before the universe was created. This energy is continuing to manifest through us as long as we are alive. It helps us have an experience of our life.

Thought is a Principle that allows us to give form to this formless and spiritual energy in a way that we create images in our minds. It's our thinking that gives us the moment-to-moment experience of life. For example, if you are having a moment of bother, that feeling of bother is being created by the Principle of Thought. If you are having a moment of joy, that's coming to you from within via the power you have to create your thinking about life.

That was very helpful for me to see because prior to understanding this particular Principle, I would blame my experiences on something outside of me like my wife, friends, boss or job. They are the reason I'm bothered, annoyed or joyful and so on. This understanding of the Principles, particularly the Principle of Thought – when I really saw that through insight – brought me to look within to where my experience was coming from. Not to look at my particular thinking and try to do something about my particular thinking, but to move within myself to see that I am part of this energy that created the way I'm experiencing my boss, work, wife, and son. That gave me freedom of thought, meaning I could see the possibility to think anyway I wanted to.

When I thought my experience was caused by other people I had no way to look beyond that because they were the reason, so if they don't fix themselves I'm going to have to feel the same thing constantly in their presence when they act a certain way. The beauty of looking at this Principle of Thought is that it had me look within, not to my thinking, but deeper. I saw the fact that I'm a thinker and that's what is creating the experience I'm having now which led to the freedom to think any way I wanted to think about that issue. This is what has helped me move beyond my conditioning.

One other thing. Understanding the Principle of Mind – our true nature, what we truly are, this spiritual energy – helped me see along the way that we're not a personality, we're not a fixed entity because we can transcend the way we have learned to be in life. So if you are someone who grew up learning to be a worrier, you're not wedded to that personality once you understand where your experience is coming from. When you really have an insight into where your experience is coming from, you can transcend that habit of worrying. You're not fixed, you're not wedded to the learning that took place as you grew up.

The Principle of Consciousness is the energy that allows us to become aware of life, to become aware of what we've created through the power of Thought. It brings awareness to us so that we actually can have an experience of what we're creating through Thought. We can experience our thinking because of Consciousness – it brings our thinking to life. With the Three Principles, every moment we are manifesting this energy and that formless energy is created into an experience we become aware of through Thought and Consciousness.

My suggestion for people wanting to understand the Three Principles is to stay reflective – don't try to understand these Principles.You don't want to try to get an intellectual understanding of what I'm saying here because I'm doing my best to point to something that you cannot find in the real world, in the physical world. If what I'm saying resonates with you, let that sit with you and let it percolate so you find your own understanding.

When I first heard about the Principles, I didn't understand them. I really had no sense of what they meant. I just stayed reflective with what little thing made sense to me. What did I see that resonated for me? I read Sydney Banks' books that pointed to them and just continued to stay reflective. At that time, surprisingly, I had insights into the Principles. Now it's not surprising that our evolution to understanding the

Principles comes through realisations – a learning we are not really aware of – we can realise knowledge through insights. We have that capacity as well as learning things intellectually. That's how you want to take in your understanding of the Principles, especially if it's new to you. See if anything I've shared here resonates with you and let that percolate. That's how I would go about it as you read all of these chapters if this understanding of the Principles is new for you.

How do you describe the work you do with clients?

I see the work as helping people find an understanding. Whether it's as a coach or therapist it means the work is to guide people to their own understanding of what they truly are and also where their experience comes from. What it isn't is giving strategies and methods to reach some goal, for me this is about an understanding that takes place within our clients.

What's the driver behind the way you work with clients? Your philosophy?

All of my clients have all they are looking for within them and we are all the same spiritual energy using Thought and Consciousness to create a reality we live in. When I'm with someone, that's my driving stance or the place I sit, knowing that my clients are the same as me. They have all the knowledge they are looking for within them and we are connected to the same spiritual energy. No matter how they are showing up in front of me I sit in that knowing and we're kind of in a partnership talking to one another to see where the insights take place, either with my client or me as we are talking together. That's what I sit in, knowing we are the same spiritual energy. That helps me because people show up in all different kinds of ways and with all different kinds of problems and that can, in a way, be distracting. What helps me with that is to just see that we are connected right now and try to speak to that intelligence that we are a part of and let that guide us.

If there was one thing you could tell your younger self about working with clients, what would it be?

For me, starting out from this understanding, it would be to continue being thrilled to have found something that is helpful and stay thrilled about it. Don't get caught up with thinking how you are doing or comparing yourself to other people that you admire. Just keep sharing with people what you know to be true. Stay with that feeling of discovery.

For me, the 38 years I've had with the Principles has always led to more and more discovery so I would say: stay with that feeling of wanting to share with people and the excitement you have about what you've seen and just talk from there. I think the only way we lose it is when we start thinking about whether we are teaching well or whether we are doing it like other people who have been doing it longer than us. If we stay away from evaluating ourselves and stay in the feeling of discovery, we will continue to evolve our understanding and also we'll evolve the way we work from this understanding.

Do you prepare for a client session and if so, how?

This is really valuable and important to me because I believe there is something you do. When I started to lead trainings internationally, in the UK (at the time I started the trainer group in London) there was a book out that was popular called *Do Nothing* and so the group was talking about there is nothing to do when you coach.

For example, I told the group that when I entered the room to meet with them I got out of my personal thinking. I looked to get into the feeling of this understanding and the feeling of being with this group of people – the loving feelings I have – and that I wanted to sit in the spirit of being of service to them. So that's what I do, I do that with every session, really get to the feeling of this understanding and out of my own thinking.

Before coming to a session I may have had to drive through traffic or I may not have had a good morning leaving the house and so I have to get those things out of my head and get to the deeper feeling of being of service to my clients. I don't think of myself doing that any more, I just do it. I get into a welcoming feeling, being of service to something greater than me. Probably through the whole session I am adjusting and trying to drop any kind of personal thinking that comes in during the session.

So, in terms of doing, I do that because I think it makes sense to be out of your own personal thinking when you are with another human being or with a group who wants to learn from you. You have to be able to get to the feeling of connectedness with the group or the individual. I also think that requires adjustments around your day of client work, you can't keep your personal thinking out of your head, but you can adjust to come back to the deeper feeling of being of service. That first training group really saw that they wanted to get to that feeling of being of service and also get out of their own personal thinking. A lot of people call that presence, but it is something to do when you go online or you enter your office. You want to move away from it being all about yourself and into that deeper feeling of love and understanding, being of service, this deeper essence.

What's your intention with a client, if any? Are you trying to get them to see anything?

For me, my intention for the session is to really be in rapport and listen and let the listening guide me. I want people I work with to find their own way, to have their own realisations and insights about their true nature and how, for me anyway, the Three Principles operate through them.

I want people to come up with their own realisations for what fits for them in terms of the way they share and their own listening process. So overall, I would think that's my intention, but I don't have an intention in the session. I let my listening guide me because in my work with the Principles, the logic is that when you are working with people as a coach, a mentor or therapist, there's the intelligence of Mind there to guide you. My intention is to try and hear that and come back to that, really come back to that.

Overall, I want to make sure my clients have their own realisations and I'm always looking to see that they can bring that into their own lives and sustain it. In each session I go in trying to connect on that deep level and listen as best I can.

Is there a process to your client work? Components?

I started in 1983 meeting Sydney Banks and listening to him at seminars, before there were the Principles actually. There was a small group of us in the San Francisco Bay area at that time. George and Linda Pransky were here, so I would meet with George every Tuesday and we would have coffee and talk about the understanding. I think through the first year or two together we kind of looked at a way to go about sharing this understanding. At first we just looked at giving people a nice feeling, talking about what we were learning from Sydney Banks and some understanding of thought. What we discovered was that if you didn't tell people where their experience was coming from they would attribute it to other things outside of themselves. They would come back and say, "I started to bring crystals" (nothing against this I'm just making the point) and use them to get the feeling more or read the Bible or read other things, etc. What we realised was that we still needed to talk about what Syd was saying more clearly than just give people a good feeling.

So through my years of mentoring, including the 18 years in San José, California with the Three Principles Division, I developed some ideas around how to go about it. The first thing being that you want to share what you know, that's it, stay with what you know. That will continue to evolve. So each time you share you want to be sure you know it's what you know at the time, not some idea you had the other day. I will periodically drift from what I know and once I recognise that I will tell my clients, "Ooh you know what; I really didn't have a feeling for that, let's go back, sorry about that, I was kind of talking from my intellect so I want to go back and hear again what you were saying so I could really share what I know". No big deal, but you really want to honour that and continue to evolve your understanding.

The other thing I noticed along the way is if you don't have rapport, that feeling of connection in you and that other person, and if you're not listening deeply enough, your teaching/sharing doesn't go well. Clients really don't listen to you. I started to see that it was valuable to get the rapport first and really let the listening guide you. Then when you share it's almost a no brainer. I saw that point for me when I was sharing. If I would just start out when somebody asked me what would be helpful and I started to share what I knew, plus the rapport wasn't right, it just didn't go well. People would blank out, be resistant or challenge me, so I realised I'd better work at getting rapport first. Sometimes that takes a number of sessions depending on how open people are or how insecure people are. You get it, then you lose it, you get it, then you lose it.

So I found that process to really be helpful to me. I don't think about that consciously but if something is off in the session or the relationship, I kind of look to rapport and listening. Maybe I need to go back and look at rapport or I quiet down and look at my listening.

That's the process that has kind of been my foundation but mainly it's about making sure that what I'm sharing is true for me today. I'm not always going to be on that and if it doesn't really go well I just step back, get that truth for me and share again because it's human to human. Whenever I have adjusted with clients and I'm talking and I really don't feel like I know this right now, I'll say something like "I don't want to continue talking to you at this level, I want to make sure that what I'm saying to you is true for me today, is it okay if we go back?" Every person has supported that. Why? Because you are human, people hear that in you and that's the feeling in you, the truth in you that makes this client work powerful, very, very powerful. People have always supported that. That's my process, I look to that as my guide.

What I learned through the years is I would get insecure about going in without really knowing too much and I would pull on something I had seen the week before and it didn't do much. Now what I would say is that, if you are in that connection, the intelligence of Mind may give you what you taught yesterday but it will have a different feeling from if you just use that repetitively. It's not like you don't use a story that you have used before or an insight you used before, but when it occurs to you from the connection you have made with the group, it's different, it's alive today.

Do you go into reflection before a session?

You could say that one of the aspects of the energy you sit in is reflection. It's really staying open to what you are hearing and kind of letting that sit with you. It's moment to moment, we are kind of describing an in-the-now experience, it's kind of more reflection than being active. Seeing what comes through you and how it fits. The foundation we've talked about with this question is kind of like a dance. You listen and something comes to you and you share and you listen to that and that guides you further. So it's always that balance. When any of that is not in balance, you listen to that and make an adjustment. It's always that.

When I share I'm always listening: "How did it go? Did that make sense to you? How did that make sense to you?" That relationship together guides it to a moment where there is potential to share something and someone could get an insight.

For example, I was just in Winnipeg, Canada, where I did some training this past weekend. Somebody was asking me a question about, "You say this and it says this in the Principles, and then you say this, and then you say that". As I listened to this participant, I got curious, "Why are you making the difference?" He said something, but it didn't feel like he answered it so I said, "You saw this so why are you asking about the different way I said it?" All of a sudden it came to him that he was listening to me trying to understand precisely. I said, "That's where the problem is, you are thinking too much and want to get this precisely". And bingo, he had this tremendous insight that freed him up. Through the rest of the training he would kid about that. He would comment, "I just want to get this precisely" and everybody would laugh. He started getting these deep insights where all of a sudden he would just start laughing from the freedom of having to get this precisely.

There's no right way to do this?

You find your own way and you just learn from one another. I remember many, many years ago that Elsie Spittle spoke at this programme we were doing in San Jose, California. She talked about listening, it was different to the way I talked about listening and it just helped me see more. You start to see that people go about it differently, but they are in that feeling and they are speaking the truth of what they saw of what Sydney Banks is pointing us towards. What I think they are not doing is teaching their concepts and ideas because it's so easy to take ideas that come to you and teach those, it gets a little away from the deeper feeling from where those ideas came from.

I have seen other people share and talk about their own process and they are doing it differently, but they are staying true to something deep in them, they are staying true to the feeling. Through my years of sharing I was really fortunate because when I first heard Syd and had that insight, I was meeting with clients five to six hours per day, five days a week for many, many years. I was forced to go back to the drawing board and really stay with the truth of this understanding. I love that because it really taught me to trust the intelligence of Mind, plus it’s a discovery, an ongoing discovery. You’re not going to get it perfect or precise ever, it’s learning everyday, it’s learning every session, it's learning for the rest of your career.

What happens within you if you get into trouble with a client? What do you do?

What happens for me is I have to quiet myself down. When I notice I’m off in what I’m sharing, or my clients don’t look like they're connected, or they're challenging, whatever it can be, I have to quiet down. I just have to go to a quiet place inside of me and see what comes next. I stop everything, drop everything and go back inside of me and get quiet. That’s it.

What I see most of the time is that it’s a partnership. I have to get quiet and listen to the guidance and it might be that I need to get rapport again, it might be I have to listen deeper, it might be I have to apologise, or it might be I have to tell my client what happened. Whatever it is, it’s human to human and the wisdom is there to guide you.

Here's a story because there are two ways of looking at this. There were times, throughout my many years of working with clients, where later on after a session that I felt didn't go well I saw what happened – maybe on my drive home, maybe an hour later – and now I could make an adjustment and learn from it. Sometimes when that happened and the session went poorly, I called my client and said I didn't think the session went well or sometimes I waited for the next session to tell them. I was surprised sometimes that clients would say they got a lot out of that session.

One time I was with someone who was recovering from alcohol addiction and they were big time into the Alcoholics Anonymous community. This was 25 years ago. This person said something from the AA programme and I immediately responded that it didn't fit the Principles, that really wasn't the Principles and right away the feeling left the room, right away we were disconnected and I just had to quieten down. I was feeling insecure, I had to get out of all that and get quiet and just get the feeling back.

So what came to me was that I knew he had grandchildren so I asked how his grandkids were and we were talking about how they were doing and all of a sudden the feeling came back and we started to feel connected again. Then it came to me, you need to apologise. I apologised for the way I talked to him and I saw, as I was apologising, that there was wisdom in what he was saying. I said, "Sorry about the way I came across, I really hear there was wisdom in what you were trying to convey and that the wisdom helped you and all I wanted to share with you was how to look at that through the Principles, can we go back to that?" By then the feeling was right, the intelligence had guided me to be human and we were able to talk in a different way. I was more accepting, rather than saying there is a right way to see this. Once that came across and we got the feeling, we could have a nice conversation together about what wisdom he saw and how that might fit the understanding I wanted to share with him.

Most of the time when I feel it's off, I have to get quiet. I have to get out of my thinking and regroup around that feeling in me and then I get guided about what to do next. It makes sense, doesn't it? If it goes wrong, you as a coach or therapist are probably into some thinking and so is your client, but you have to take responsibility to get yourself back first, then you can help your client.

Is problem solving for a client the end of the story? Or do you go further?

I do not view the Three Principles approach as a problem solving approach. My work is to bring an understanding to my clients. That is, I want clients to experience a rise in their level of consciousness, their understanding if you will. Of course clients come to me with life problems or areas of themselves they wish to change or improve. However, my focus is to provide a direction that leads clients to gain realisation or insight into the knowledge of life that exists within their consciousness. Once clients experience a rise in consciousness they have new or "wise thoughts" that allow them to take care of any issue in a way that is right for them. This is the hope of the Principles. Clients can reach a level of consciousness whereby they transcend problems. Clients can live beyond their conditioning or learned habits of thought.

During my numerous years of working in the field of addictions, I have been blessed to see many clients gain a level of consciousness where they transcend their addictions. Again, this is the hope of the Principles in that it allows clients to live at a level of consciousness that brings contentment, wisdom, love and understanding that is beyond the level of suffering at which addictions or other life problems exist.

Is the feeling important for you when working with clients?

It's probably the ultimate guide. You can't really describe it, but it's love and understanding. It's just this deep essence. People describe it in many different ways when you are working together.

It could be a partnership, people sometimes liken it to talking to a friend out on the back porch. It's just this deep feeling, that to me, is a space you are in where there is this beautiful feeling of connection, of love and understanding, of knowing we are spiritual.

It isn't that I think that, it's that I'm trying to describe a feeling that's hard to talk about. It's not personal. That's why you can talk about this feeling of love and understanding and be a very responsible coach/therapist because it's not personal, it's not romantic love, it's not wanting this person to be your friend kind of love, it's this deep essence. In that feeling there is everything you need in order to help someone, to guide someone or to be of service to someone.

I guess that's my guide really, when my feeling is off, like we just talked about, I have to make an adjustment and get it back. So that's my guide. It is the feeling in me. If I get judgmental, or if I start to categorise someone or I start to get impatient, I'm off and I notice the feeling is off and I have to go back and get it.

Another story that goes back to the question about trouble. I was coaching a group about relationships with this understanding, I was talking and all of a sudden the feeling was off in me. I realised that I was just talking intellectually, I was using something I had taught another group last week and so I had to get quiet. That's what I do, I get quiet. I'm quiet, I can't find anything and it occurred to me that the group needs to know why I was quiet and so I told them. I said, "You know I started to talk to you about this but it just wasn't right for you and I'm getting quiet to find something new to share with you, is that okay with you?" And all of them said, "Yeah, just do that". Well lo and behold, the minute I checked back in with myself I had something to share and so I started to share something that was new, it had a feeling with it and I was back in the feeling, the intelligence gave me something to share and it was a wonderful session. Just trusting that this feeling is the most important part of you and not start to share until you have it. I always use it as a guide.

Could you share a story or stories of what worked well and what didn't and what are the takeaways?

I've had a lot of both. If you can imagine the number of hours and the number of people I've seen, I'm talking to groups weekly for five to six hours. There are times I taught and it just offended people, it didn't hit the mark. I knew people left and they really weren't happy with what happened in the conversation. Then others had beautiful, beautiful insights throughout the years that they have gathered. I think the only thing you have to see is a calling. If you are really feeling you want to work with people and you really see this spiritual understanding has given you something and you want to share that, that's a calling. You are being called.

You don't want to worry about how well you are doing. You are going to have times where you don't know what to say, you are going to have times where you don't listen well, you are going to have times when somebody is presenting so intensely that you are thrown by it. But remember, if you go back, whatever point that is, whether in a session or afterwards, and just get to that neutral feeling, you'll see what to do next, it will help you.

When I mentored a group I was training, there was one person who shared something and I replied to her in a way that made her feel wrong. Luckily it was lunchtime, I had just started to get insecure, I didn't know what to do. As I left and went to lunch, two things came to me. I could go back and not deal with it and the training would go okay and I also knew if I didn't go back and put this right, this training would be okay, but it wouldn't be deep because the group heard this. But I'm still insecure! So I just relax my mind, quiet down and I saw the guidance to go back and apologise and talk it out with that person.

I went back and did that. The group met and I went to that person and said, "I'm so sorry for the way I talked with you earlier, I really don't want us to feel bad with each other, I want to hear what you were asking so I can do a better job?" The whole thing went deep. The whole group went deep. She connected with me and asked a question and I saw what I could share and we just had a wonderful group the rest of the time. After that training, she actually wanted to work more with me. I didn't know this ahead of time of course, but do you see the process? You're not going to feel good if something is off, just relax your mind, the wisdom will guide you. It's always about going back to your humanness, it's always going to be about capturing the fact that you're being human with someone. Usually it's about explaining what happened within you and reaching out to make it better.

What I think is most valuable is not to worry about it going wrong. What's most important is to see you have a calling, you're not always going to be "right on" in your sessions, but if you are human and go back to the love and understanding for your clients, that will take care of you and that will make it right. It really is a calling. I don't know why, for you or for your audience, why we heard this, but we are called to this and you get back to that feeling.

Chapter Thirteen

Annika Hurwitt PhD

"Everyone is looking to find their way back home"
Sydney Banks

How do you describe the work you do with clients?

I help people realise that, just like everything else in nature, we are part of a pre-existing spiritual system. In nature we find repeating patterns such as fractals and the fibonacci series, which are found in the trees, the rocks and the flowers, and these patterns are designed so that everything in nature thrives and functions at its best. These patterns are spiritual in nature – because they're discovered, not created by human beings. Human beings also have a repeating pattern built into us, also spiritual in nature, to help us maintain our psychological balance, thrive, and evolve. That pattern is the Three Principles of Mind, Consciousness and Thought. These Principles are what gives rise to the human experience. When you realise this, it allows your mind to calm itself, achieve natural mental presence, and become resilient. This gives you the ability to heal psychologically and begin to enjoy life; to have ongoing mental clarity and wellbeing.

What are The Three Principles?

The Three Principles are Mind – a formless energy that powers up all of life; Thought – which powers up the thinking we create; and Consciousness – which gives you the ability to experience your thinking.

What's the driver behind the way you work with clients? Your philosophy?

My philosophy is that people are innately psychologically healthy – that like everything else in nature we were designed perfectly to evolve and thrive. Becoming aware of the Principles of Mind, Consciousness and Thought, and that we have a built-in GPS system called our feelings to show you when you are out of alignment with these Principles and when you are in alignment with them, allows people to bring themselves out of psychologically challenging states and get back on track with life. So many people are working so hard to try to fix their thinking, and they are so discouraged because they can't do it. Of course they can't – we have too many thoughts going on all the time, and most of them are unconscious. That's why the discovery of a pre-existing system called The Three Principles is so significant. That's what drives me, that's the understanding behind my work.

If there was one thing you could tell your younger self about working with clients, what would it be?

Ever since I started teaching The Principles I've felt completely taken care of. I knew I had been given all I needed because the results I saw in people were incredible. The only thing I can think of to say is for quite a long time before I was introduced to these Principles I was really searching hard to find the link between the psychological and the spiritual. I would say to that person, just be patient, you are going to find it, it really does exist, and when you find it everything will change.

From the beginning, as a Three Principles coach and therapist, things just worked out for me. I had a successful psychotherapy practice before that, but I knew that there was more to life than helping people fix their thinking. So I would tell that younger coach that it's coming, just be patient.

Do you prepare for a client session and if so, how?

It really depends. It's interesting. When I started with the Principles, if I was doing an intensive I would spend a lot of time reflecting on the client and seeing what it felt like they needed next and listening for insights. I would really clear my schedule completely so I had lots of empty space. But over time, doing intensives and receiving insights about the clients I work with became second nature.

Now it naturally weaves itself into my days when I am doing an intensive, although I cut my schedule way back so I have plenty of time. Mind, Thought and Consciousness take care of you, so if I have a client I'm working with, not in an intensive, if there is something that I need to add to the next session, it comes to me. The thoughts and insights will keep coming to mind, and then I will just listen, listen to the unknown for what it is and I'll act on it.

What's your intention with a client, if any? Are you trying to get them to see anything?

My intention is to be of service, full stop. Whatever they need shows up.

Is there a process to your client work? Components?

Yes, in almost every session, I listen for a little while and that creates rapport with the client as well as giving me needed information. Then I introduce the idea of Principles – that they exist, and that we already know about them from our physical existence, as with gravity. They are very natural and very instinctive, and very much below our radar – we don't think about them. Then I introduce these Principles, and I explain that there is also a set of feelings that show when we are out of alignment with them and in alignment with them. This gives us a roadmap, so when you get those feeling indicators that you are out of alignment, that realisation brings about a natural re-alignment with these Principles. This gives people a very tangible way to see the Principles in action. I do that in the first session almost every time. I explain it in subsequent sessions until people see it more deeply.

What happens within you if you get into trouble with a client? What do you do?

If I feel like I'm getting in trouble and I'm losing my balance, or I'm getting insecure or frightened, I just listen more deeply. "Help me out here", you know, "I feel like I'm not really connecting with what you are saying". I listen more deeply to what they are saying, and I listen for the feeling behind the words. Stop, re-group, check in with them. Usually through attention and good listening, we get back on track. If I feel lost or get insecure, I realise I'm out of alignment with these Principles and look to have the realisation that yes, once again, I'm feeling my thoughts about the client, not the client without the mediation of my own thinking. Once that realisation happens, I settle down and get good ideas on how to navigate the session.

Is problem solving for a client the end of the story? Or do you go further?

I don't problem solve. The end of the story is when the client feels grounded in this understanding, and knows that they understand what it's like to be in alignment with these Principles, and with their psychological health. Also knowing when they're not, and how to continue to align with the Principles. That's the end of our time together. They solve their own problems.

Is the feeling important for you when working with clients?

Not really. There is a feeling of rapport and not rapport, but beyond that not really. Feelings are important because they are our GPS system, they show us whether we are caught in an illusion that life, not thought, is creating our psychological experience in the moment. When people learn this, they know when they're out of alignment with these Principles, and how to find their way back home. The result is that they become grounded in the present most of the time. They have much less insecurity. It's very freeing.

Could you share a story or stories of what worked well and what didn't and what are the takeaways for you?

Last year I had a new client. She was clinically depressed, in her 50's. Part of what triggered it was that she moved to the Boston area from another state. She was away from her grown-up daughter for the first time, and because of the move her husband was working about an hour away in Boston, He had to stay there during the week because it was too long of a commute. Maybe it was one and a half hours. She was very lonely for the first time in her life, and she had sunk into such a depression, she couldn't get off the couch most days.

There isn't much to this story. I taught her what I teach everybody else which I've described already. By the second session she was feeling better, by the third session she was getting up and out. She had horses that she never visited and now she was back in the barn. At the fourth session she said don't call me, I'll call you. I haven't heard from her again. She was diagnosed with clinical depression. I see people get over depression all the time which is one of the miracles of this work, but four sessions – it might even have been three! I guess the takeaway is just keep it pure and never assume anything. She was completely cured.

In my experience, if people are ready they learn this and if not, they don't. It has become more clear over the years that when you learn this you get on a path of spiritual evolution as well as psychological healing and evolution – and not everybody is ready for that. It's like we are all walking around asleep and some of us are ready for that little tap – then say, "Oh yes I'm so interested in that". And some people just aren't.

As I've moved around so much in recent years, I actually put an ad in *Psychology Today* for the first time after having been a psychotherapist and coach for 35 years. Most of my coaching is referral based, but sometimes I get people from that ad who know nothing about this. So they are the real testing pool. In some ways it's more fascinating because out of the people who come to me about 85% are ready and they hear this and they say, "Wow, we are so lucky we found you". And about 15% say thank you very much, and I don't see them again. I guess what I've learned from that is not to take it personally – people are ready when they're ready.

Really if I look back before that stage of my evolution as a coach and therapist, probably the biggest mistakes I ever made were not listening deeply enough to people or being presumptuous that I should just teach them this. So I've learned to really listen now and get permission before I teach the Principles; I want to teach you this, do you want to hear about it? Sometimes people say no. It's rare. Those are the people that usually end up not being my clients, but sometimes they just need a little more rapport building.

So probably the biggest lesson for me has been in listening, which is another aspect of being present to what is actually happening in the room and not just, here I go, I'll say the things that I say!

Chapter Fourteen

Judith Sedgeman EdD

"If you take on someone else's belief to replace a belief of your own, you may experience a temporary placebo effect, but you have not found a lasting answer. However, if you replace an old belief with a realization from your own inner wisdom, the effect and results are superior and permanent."

The Missing Link by Sydney Banks

What does coaching from the Three Principles or being a Three Principles coach mean to you as in the definition?

What it means to me is being the best I can be, and getting better all the time because coaching is both mentoring and learning. You can only share what you have. I learned early on that there is a definition out in the world that assumes coaching is a body of knowledge that coaches have and they transmit that. It echoes the educational system, where the idea is that the teacher knows everything and the students are the empty vessels and you just pour a lot of information into them. Actually, from the Three Principles perspective it's not like that at all. It's the exact opposite of that. Coaching is realising that the person you are sitting across from has within them everything you have; there is no difference between us, but they haven't necessarily seen deeply into their own spirit, their own soul, their own capacity. So we explore that together.

From insecurity, people look for a methodology. The source of the traditional method is that clients are insecure about whether they know enough and teachers or coaches are insecure about their own fund of knowledge. In the Principles world, on the other hand, we know that everyone has access to the same wisdom and creativity. So coaching is helping people discover what they don't realise they already know, and don't realise the fact of wisdom – fresh ideas that come to us when we need them. But a coach can't point to something he or she has never seen, so the happier we are, the deeper we go within ourselves, the more we learn, the more we really listen to our clients and learn from them, learn what's missing for them, the better it gets for us and our clients.

What's the driver behind the way you work with clients? Your philosophy?

At the deepest level, it is just wanting peace on earth and wanting people to see the beauty in each other and the spiritual nature of life. The essence of our client work is to see the beauty and resiliency in other people no matter what they think is wrong with them or what's going on. If people weren't unknowingly insecure, we wouldn't have the problems we have in the world.

To me working with clients from the inside-out, is the way people get inspired out of insecurity, and once they see it in themselves they see it in other people. So if you produce a generation of coaches, counsellors and therapists who come from love and understanding and see the beauty in people, you would just continually regenerate the feeling that other people are fascinating and wonderful and we are all the same, and differences are just thoughts – all the understanding that helps people come to peace with things. At the bottom of all that I do, "What is the driver?" It's the desire for peace on earth and for love and understanding to replace insecurity, fear and distrust.

Would that be the same as the WAY you work?

I don't know if this is relevant, but I had a call from a person who was interested in mentoring with me. This person had been through a big coaching programme and he was so insecure about trying to do it. It seemed like when he was in the programme he was swept up in it and everybody practising on each other as they do and helping each other as they do and suddenly he was out in the world on his own looking at a client and he felt inadequate and unprepared. He wasn't sure where to start.

I told him generally I just start by listening to the client and asking what they are looking for, and I come from curiosity and caring. He said, "Who would pay for that, you can get that from your Grandmother!" I said, "I am a Grandmother, people pay for it, so what can I say?"

The fact that is completely new to people, is the idea that a coach wouldn't just come on strong and say, "Okay I have analysed your situation and these are the things we are going to work on". Really that's selling the client short and selling yourself short because every time you meet with the client, both you and the client see something new. You want to start with a clear head, and see where the session takes you.

I look at it as a fresh start every time we meet and start from curiosity. What is on that person's mind today, how are they thinking as they are describing their questions, what are they looking for that they aren't seeing yet? I don't tell them what it is because what would that do for them? You tell somebody what's wrong with them and they say "yeah, yeah, I already knew that" but when they SEE it fresh for themselves, then they have gone somewhere new and they say, for example, "Oh my gosh, I never actually realised that I get intimidated by business clients", well that's a big thing to realise because it becomes meaningless once you see it. I would say that's it, curiosity and love, and waiting for the moment of wisdom that helps me point in a direction that opens their eyes to something. When they see it, it changes for them. Barriers to their own life and work just fade away.

If there was one thing you could tell your younger self about working with clients, what would it be?

What I would tell my younger self is: Shut up and listen! Really! Because in the beginning you get enthused and sometimes you jump right in. You learn patience over time, the longer you listen, the deeper you go. I think when I was younger and starting out I would get a thought – you know the person would be talking and I would be listening for a little while and then something would occur to me – and I would leap right into it. I don't do that anymore, I listen longer and talk less in the beginning. I probably talk as much, if you took it in total, as I ever did, but I don't talk first. I don't just jump in. That's really what I would tell my younger self, shut up and listen, be patient, don't just roll with your first thoughts and dominate the session and then lose your chance to get deeper with the client and watch them blossom as their insights emerge.

Do you prepare for a client session and if so, how?

Yes and no. Yes in the sense that I do my best not to be distracted, to be present and not have a lot of stuff on my mind. So I don't run to the grocery store, put half my groceries away and turn on my computer because I'm almost late for a session and wonder if my ice cream is melting. I try to keep myself in a state of mind that supports caring for other people rather than being distracted by my own life. That would be my best preparation. I get everything I need to get done so I can sit down, quiet my mind and be at peace when I'm ready to talk to someone.

Also, as I work with people I try to build. I pay attention to things that people have talked about before that they are still baffled about, or struggling with, and go back and ask them if anything has been resolved, what has occurred to them, and so on. So I try to start with better questions over time, reflecting on where we are and where we've been. I don't really prepare notes or anything like that, I don't say we are going to do this and this because I don't know where the client is until the client is in front of me. I never know when a client may get on a call and say, "OMG I had this amazing inspired thought!" and it's so fabulous that it just erases all the problems they appeared to have had, so you are starting with a whole new person. I always try to build from their inspiration.

What's your intention with a client, if any? Are you trying to get them to see anything?

My goal with all my clients is to help them to find peace of mind, and then get in touch with their own wisdom and insight, their own spiritual nature. Then I explain to them what happened if they don't realise they are doing better because they just found a peaceful state of mind and solved their own problems, answered their own questions. That's it. It's always unknown the path we'll follow, but that's always the destination.

Is there a process to your client work? Components?

Sort of, because I'm flexible depending on the client. I basically do a few things, like I start with people and say let's just do five sessions and I give people a break if they sign up for five because my experience over time is that they are either really getting somewhere in five sessions or I'm not a good fit for them. I don't want to have people hanging around if they are not getting anything from our work together. I'll refer them to somebody else because there are tons of wonderful people out there and it doesn't belong to us, it belongs to the universe. So I will do five, and if they are making great progress I'll do another few or five sessions if the client wants more.

A lot of my clients will do five and I don't hear from them for a couple of months and then they get into their work and they'll call me back and say, "Can I get a tune up?" I'll hear from people from time to time and they'll want another five or they'll have a client they want me to sit in with, or a child they want me to talk to, and that kind of thing. So I'm very flexible with my processes and I try to take it incrementally depending on the clients' needs.

What happens within you if you get into trouble with a client? What do you do?

I stop and I say, "I'm really sorry because what I just said is not helpful, let's just take a moment". And I'll chat with them about anything for a bit. It gets us both reset to start over. I'm not ashamed to say I blew it, because that's something people need to learn. People are very forgiving. If people are going to pay you, they want you to succeed, so if you are going off track and they know it too, it's obvious to everybody, and you're willing to say, "Time out – I just completely blew that and I'm getting way off in a direction that we don't need to go and I just need to take a deep breath", usually they are very co-operative and they are grateful. It gives them a model to follow in their own work.

Afterwards we will talk about that anybody can do that, it's easy to say I'm sorry. It's hard to keep going like a bull in a china shop and pretend you know what you are doing when you don't. The answer is always in stopping, and going to quiet. Together we learn to have faith in quietude and trusting wisdom to guide us back on course. I've had a couple of times when I've really lost the client and I've said, "Look I'm not going to charge you for this call and let's schedule another to replace it". It's part of doing business.

I was in a restaurant with my daughter where we ordered something that we didn't think we would like to share as an appetiser, and the waiter was just into it, and he wouldn't stop suggesting it, and he insisted we would love it. Well we didn't like it and the waiter who had done this big sell on us comes over to the table and sees we are not eating it and we say sorry we just don't like it. He took it away and said what would you like instead. That's it. He didn't charge us for it and he replaced it. That's good customer service: he thought it was going to be great, it didn't turn out great, let's just start over.

Is problem solving for a client the end of the story? Or do you go further?

They have to solve the problem, I wouldn't solve the problem. It wouldn't matter if I saw the perfect solution, I wouldn't even mention it because that would be my solution if I had that problem. It's not going to help them. They need to realise they can and will see their own solutions.

For example, if I get someone who is coaching and they say, I was with this client and I thought we were going to talk about this and they veered off and this other thing came up and I got freaked out because I didn't know what to say about it and blah, blah ... that would look like the problem to them. My feeling is that my job in the session is to get the client quietened down and to stop judging themself to realise that everybody makes mistakes and we all get off track and we all get to the point where we can't quite see it yet. Then they can see that maybe the solution to that perceived problem is to step back, listen deeper, enquire, be willing to not know, take your time, let your client talk some more until you get some clarity.

Quite often somebody brings something up, especially if they are upset about it, and you want to leap right in. Solving the problem for my client, in this example, would be for them to see by the end of the session that they just got insecure, jumped in too fast and didn't ask enough questions. We might even role play that a little bit. That's not the end of the road because that resolves their immediate question. It doesn't take them deep enough to not replicate that problem, so the next step after that would be to go deeper to see clearly that doesn't happen if you recognise your own insecurity, don't let it trick you into circular thinking and quick action.

It's okay to have an insecure thought while we're working with clients, we all do, but we all know acting on our insecure thoughts doesn't work out in life and it doesn't work out in our practice either. So if my insecure thought is, "OMG I have never thought of this problem before and now I don't know what to say", that's my insecurity and has nothing to do with the client. I have to get calm enough to let that go and just keep listening until I see something. So the deeper point would be for the practitioner to truly feel that there are no insurmountable problems, that wisdom will always serve us, and that the client's wisdom will always come to the surface when we both quiet down. That would be the deeper learning for any problem.

Are your clients always Three Principles coaches or practitioners?

Yes, I choose it that way at this point in my life. When I started out I worked with all kinds of people and would work in companies on all kinds of topics. I did things like strategic thinking seminars and teamwork and things like that. I don't travel as much as I used to and I don't do big corporate trainings – they all want somebody young who is going to dance on the table (laughs), I'm past that point not that I have never done it, but not recently. I tend to work with people who are dedicated to working with the Three Principles almost exclusively.

I mostly work with people who have seen how life works and they are working to help other people see it. My clientele at this point in my life tends to be people who have been involved with the Principles for at least three or four years and maybe they have gone through some other courses and seminars and they are looking to go as deep as they can and they really feel like they still have blindspots and blocks, which we all do. I am trying to work with people that want to be as deep as they can coming from the Three Principles; that's my preferred clientele now.

Is the feeling important for you when working with clients?

Yes, it's actually everything. I was surprised how it can happen online. I was a little dubious at first to do long distance coaching on Zoom. I was thinking that this is not the same as having the person in the room, but it actually is. I think sometimes people are even more forthcoming online because, even though you are right there, face-to-face, you're not physically in the same room, and they feel safer in their own setting, they are not sitting in your office or a hotel meeting room.

I feel like clients are just like me; they're probably wearing something nice on top and maybe wearing their shorts or their sweats and their bunny slippers and they've got their tea (laughs). So I feel like it works out fine online when people are comfortable. The feeling is the currency of the Three Principles and when it's off, everything else is just intellectual – trying to struggle through your thinking. When we're at ease and relaxed and get into the feeling, it is magical.

What does that mean to you? The feeling?

I think the feeling is quiet and the sense of mutual respect, that we are in this together, spiritually connected. Years ago, I went to a talk that Roger Mills did for a bunch of social workers and he did this scale where commiseration was at the bottom. It went up from commiseration to sympathy to compassion to equality. It's very interesting, I've done this exercise with some of my students in graduate class. They know intuitively that commiseration is a bad idea, like, "Oh yeah, if I had a problem like that I'd be p****d off too!" You're just joining the client's bad feeling.

But sympathy sounds good to them and I'd say, "Yes, but isn't sympathy a one up, one down?" Sympathy is, "I feel so sorry for you, dear, I know this must be hard for you, you poor thing". It's very condescending if people hear it as caring but not helpful, because all you are telling them is that they are weaker than you and you feel sorry for them. It doesn't offer hope for change or point to their strengths.

Compassion is good because at least it's up from sympathy, but it's still one up, one down, it's still saying I can help you here, I can step in, I'll give you some good advice. You know I really see and feel what you are going through. I'll help you come through it, you'll be fine.

When you come to people with equality, it becomes about your shared humanity, that we are all the same. It's letting the person know they are just having a human experience that others also have, and that we all have the same capacity to see beyond our "troubles" and find our own answers. I was very touched by that. Over the years as I've reflected on it, I've become more positive that that's the source of the feeling, that the client is fine, I'm no different from them and they are no different from me and what's in them is perfect, but it's covered over a little by their temporary fear that it might not be there, or their intimidation because people appear to know more than they do, or whatever it is.

To me that's the feeling, there's nothing wrong with this person, they don't need anything. It's unconditional love. They have what they need, but it's helpful if they could realise that deeper and deeper. That's the feeling to me, it's that feeling that we are in it together, it's the human race and nobody is winning. We are just people doing the best we can and we have these incredible spiritual gifts and the only thing that separates me from my clients is that I have spent nearly 40 years looking at them, trying to discover them deeper and deeper. To the degree you keep looking, you find more and more. It's infinite and always there.

Could you share a story or stories of what worked well and what didn't and what are the takeaways?

Let me start with what didn't, there are so many, but I'll pick one. I was working in La Conner a long time ago, about three years after first getting into this. I had moved to La Conner and I was working with George and Linda Pransky. They had people come for intensives for weekends. When you first started working with them, until they were certain about you and you were comfortable, you would sit in with them and then you'd start a session with one of them sitting with you so they could step in if things were going a little askew.

So for one of my first sessions, this woman came in who was in a really abusive relationship, the guy was close to murdering her, he was really violent and she was terrified. It was one of those situations where he was wealthy and she had a great life when he wasn't at home. She had a hard time imagining herself giving all that up. She's telling this story and I myself was divorced and I was thinking, you know it's not that bad once you take that step, it's okay, you find your way. So I'm thinking about myself and how I worked things out and feeling really sorry for this woman rather than listening to her. I don't remember whether it was George or Linda who was sitting in. I blurted out, "Why don't you just get divorced, it'll all work out". And the woman said, "I don't want to get divorced, I don't want to give all this up, I've got kids and they are at these fancy schools", and so on. She got argumentative and I got scared.

Fortunately "a Pransky" was there. It was just one of those horrible moments. I realised what I'd done wrong, I'd given her advice instead of listening and helping her find her own way, but I couldn't get it back. How do you take that back? I had to step aside, I had to just say look I'm sorry I said that, that was foolish and just sort of leave the room (laughs). That was a case where instead of listening to the client, I started listening to myself and listening to my story and thinking what helped me would help her instead of really staying close to the client story and listening to her heart and helping her find her own way. It was my bad habit. Every once in a while I would leap into advice mode. I was a consultant before I learned about the Principles, and it's easy to do because in consulting you always have an answer. But giving the answer is not a good idea. The point is to set your answer aside and assist them to find their answer.

So on to something that went really well. I learned a lot a few years ago when I was working with women who had been trafficked. Universally their biggest problem was extremely low self esteem because they had been used and abused by pimps, most of them for ten years or more. Some of them were saved from the streets when they were in their early twenties so the street life started in their early teens. It was hard for them to imagine anything else.

I had this one girl who had done great in her safe house and great with counselling, but she had fear of having a relationship. She didn't bring it up for a long time, first she was trying to get through going back to school, finishing her degree, getting a job, getting her life back, which she did over a year and a half; she even got her children back. She really wanted a relationship, but she avoided it because she thought if she ever told anybody she'd spent eight years working as a prostitute, working for this terrible pimp who beat her every day, she would never find a nice man.

I remember I was sitting with her – we used to meet on the patio of a Starbucks because she was out of the safe house by then. This beautiful day we are sitting on the patio of Starbucks and she is saying, "You know my past is so horrible and I realise it's over and I don't have to think about it, but if you're really in a relationship with somebody you can't lie to them. You have to tell them about your past". I remember listening to this thinking yes, you would have to tell them, you wouldn't want to pretend like it didn't happen.

So I'm listening and listening and listening and she finally said, "I would just have to explain I was a kid and I didn't know what I was getting into", and it just occurred to me to say, "You know what, you just had a really bad first job". I thought oh my gosh that's a little light-hearted for the occasion, but she laughed and said, "Yes, that's it!" I think I listened to her for so long I started to see that she just needed to lighten up about it, she was getting too serious, and something in my own wisdom just gave me that – you just had a really bad first job. Everyone has had bad jobs when they're young, but yours was worse.You don't have that job any more, you'll never have it again, you wouldn't apply for it! That put it in perspective.

About three weeks later she met a guy who was a policeman. She was taking her kids for ice cream and she met him waiting in line at the ice cream shop. He just sat down and chatted with them for a while, and they exchanged numbers and he called her. Time has passed and she didn't marry him or get serious. They just dated for a while. But it was good for her because she told him about her past and he didn't care. He said that it was a shame you were such an innocent kid when that happened. They had a really nice, fun relationship, he got on with her kids and so that re-introduced her to that world, that you can leave your past alone and just laugh at it no matter how terrible it was.

She called me a few months later and told me, "You know that bad job thing, it really helped me to see that I was not my job. I realised that I am not my job, any job. I am more than that".

In that case, I just trusted, I was listening and listening and listening to her and I really wasn't sure what to say, but I wasn't going in my own head thinking what would I say if I was in her situation, but just listening to her. Something told me to say that and I said it and it worked out. It worked out for her because her insight from it was much deeper than what I had said. She saw what she needed to see.

I've observed really great people like George (Pransky) and Bill (Pettit) and Elsie (Spittle) so many times do that with people – say things that seem pretty light-hearted or irreverent for the occasion – and I've thought OMG I can't believe they said that, but it's always right when it comes from that space of really loving the client and wanting to hear what they need and trusting it when it pops into your head.

So I've given you an example of blurting something out from your personal thinking, as in my first story of something that went wrong, versus blurting something out when you are just listening and listening with a free and clear mind, and all of a sudden something comes to you.

It must be hard to work with people who have been through that kind of trauma?

The one thing I learned to do is not to ask too much about the details of their time on the street because they weren't on the street when I was seeing them, and my goal was to get them into the present moment. There is this combination of curiosity and the idea you should know about your client that can easily pull you down into the details. I always kept my questions focused on their thinking about life, their dreams and ambitions, their interests, their hopes, their strengths. I noticed other people who work with that clientele tend to ask them a lot of questions, like what did the Johns say to you, and how would they beat you, and how would you cover the bruises so you could be attractive... there were all these details.

That's not a good idea. I would tell people I didn't want to hear about that stuff because here you are now, you're safe, we're in the living room of a house where you are safe and cared for so let's just be here, let's not talk about there, it's in the past. They were always relieved, they didn't really want to talk about it. They didn't mind talking about it, or they thought they were supposed to because that's the psychology habit, but they honestly didn't want to think about their past. I think my lack of interest in the details of their street life helped them also to let it go, to realise that that isn't who you are now, and it was never who you were as a spiritual being with innate health.

Chapter Fifteen

Rita J Shuford PhD

"Wisdom is not found in the world of form,
nor in remote corners of the globe.
Wisdom lies within our own consciousness...
Wisdom brings common sense to those who find it."
The Missing Link by Sydney Banks

What are The Three Principles?

The Three Principles – Mind, Consciousness and Thought – are the source, the building blocks of all reality and human experience. They define the operating system of every human being's mind. They are spiritual in nature, meaning formless intelligent energy. They point us to the fact that all life on this physical, material plane is spiritual essence, formless energy turned into form. Take a moment, look within and all around. Everything you see, feel, touch, sense, smell is brought into existence via one source, one truth, the Three Principles.

The Principles reveal that we live, moment to moment, from within, inside-out, via the creative power of Universal Mind, the intelligence of all life, Universal Consciousness, the ability to see, to be aware, to experience life and know the source within and Universal Thought, the ability, the power to create our own view and experience of life. The Principles are not religious in nature and yet, all religions stem from and point to this divine power.

The truth of the Three Principles being the source of all reality and human experience is the knowledge and wisdom of our soul. Realised more insightfully from within, beyond intellect/ego, we are freed naturally from believing we are at the mercy, the effect of conditions and circumstances in our life, past, present and future. We are built innately to break free of the past to live "now" with more unconditional love, wisdom, understanding and compassion for self and others.

So the good news is, moment to moment, from within our own mind using the power of Divine Thought and Consciousness we see, feel and experience life unfolding formless to form, spiritual to psychological. What we see, feel and how we react and behave is revealed as the product of our own mind and thought in the moment. Every nanosecond is a second chance to see life anew, to have wisdom, clarity and insight to guide us in a healthy direction.

The all encompassing nature of the Three Principles is invisible to the naked eye and must be and is realised from within through insight, a shift of consciousness. The natural outcome of deeper insight into the source of our individual experience is increased wellbeing, practical common sense, more harmonious relationships and increased creativity and productivity in our personal and professional lives...no matter what.

Why is insight into the truth of the Three Principles so important? People are suffering needlessly. Human suffering is perpetuated by innocently believing that our perceptions, feelings and reactions can be, and are, determined by some power/cause/force outside our own mind and thought, i.e., other people, circumstances, events and conditions in our life, past, present or possible future. This innocent misunderstanding leads to blaming and emotional and behavioural reactivity. All the while we are feeling the product of our thinking, the way we are using the gift of thought. Angry thought = angry feeling, inside-out. Realising that we are "feeling our own thinking", our use of the power of Thought and Consciousness in the moment, puts us more insightfully back in tune with the inside-out creative process. Our mind naturally lets go of thinking/feeling that it realises isn't true, helpful or needed in the moment.

For example, if it looks like my boss and co-workers have the power to determine how I feel and behave, I'm caught in a belief, a thought that is not true. I may have feelings of stress, fear, worry and possibly resentment and anger all blamed on my job, boss and co-workers. Acting on these feelings, our reactions and behaviours typically lead to problems in the workplace, i.e., emotional reactivity, lack of motivation, low productivity, ineffective communication and poor interpersonal relationships. The moment we realise, more insightfully, that our feelings are coming from our thoughts, our mind naturally begins to quiet, to clear, letting go of blaming the boss or co-workers for our feelings. We may not agree with the boss's thoughts and actions, but now, with insight, we have a more present, clear and open mind, a more healthy perspective. We feel better and have access to the wisdom and common sense needed in the situation.

Throughout this chapter I will refer to and expand on what it means in our daily lives, personal and professional, to realise the basic truth and common sense of our individual life experience. The hope and possibility, revealed by the Three Principles, for all human beings is that it is our birthright to:

- Be content and happy, unconditionally.
- Live with a sense of ease and wellbeing, free of chronic stress, worry, anxiety and depression.
- Have harmonious, peaceful relationships based on respect, love and understanding.
- Be naturally secure, resilient, and at peace knowing we have answers, common sense and wisdom within to handle life's challenges.

How do you describe the work you do with clients?

We are a team. I am a partner and a guide in a process, helping clients look within to find the answers, the wisdom and common sense they need for whatever is going on in their lives, personally and professionally.

What's the driver behind the way you work with clients? Your philosophy?

I have no doubt that my clients have the wisdom, clarity, and common sense for anything in life that might be on their plate and that they are meant to find that wisdom within themselves. It's there, it's the intelligence we are all born with that I call wisdom or spiritual intelligence. This intelligence is deep and profound but it is also very practical. It can be simple common sense in the daily living of our lives and handling of things. The Principles point us to that wisdom and clear away whatever might be getting in the way, all the thoughts and beliefs that interfere, whether about ourselves, about others, or about circumstances.

The recognition that thought is the only vehicle for having an experience of life is very powerful. It looks like something other than thought is creating our experience in the moment. That's a normal part of human development. We all pick up ideas, beliefs, concepts, insecurities, biases, etc, but they are all carried in thought and not a product of life happening to us.

Let me share a personal example. My husband died suddenly a little over three years ago. His death could look like the cause of my feelings and experiences, but thank God I know it isn't. I know he died, I have sadness that comes and goes, I miss him, but I know in the next moment I can be enjoying my life and being happy which I know is exactly what he would want. I want it too. More importantly I am the one living here on this physical plane. He's playing here in spirit, he's with me, but now it's time for me to see what this life is about on my own terms.

His death does not have the power to determine my experience or make decisions for me, that's going to come from within my own mind via the gift of Mind, Thought and Consciousness. Knowing this brings clarity. It's been an amazing growing time for me, finding myself and what's true for me, a deeper love for myself. Prior to this, it was easier to love others, to take care of others. I'm learning what true self is – the unconditional love and understanding. And not just love and understanding, but clarity for, in my case, what's next, what's the next step for me in life, in work, where I live, how I move forward.

The real coach/therapist/counsellor is our inner wisdom, that's the real guide and that's where I point people. Knowing that in any moment anyone can have the insights, the clarity that will help them move forward.

If there was one thing you could tell your younger self about working with clients, what would it be?

Trust yourself and be patient with yourself. Know that it's okay not to know and be okay hanging out in the unknown. Don't try to force or make up something, which I have done many times in my life. There's a feeling that comes with making something up that's not genuine. It has more of an intellectual quality of trying to fix something or explain something or analyse something. These words can take up air space and sound good, but nothing is really happening at the deeper level. Nothing happens inside the client.

I think as a young therapist sometimes the idea of hanging out in the unknown and just listening was scary. What was my client going to think? I should say something. I didn't see there was power in not knowing. A number of years ago, I finally got more comfortable. I still try to know when I don't know sometimes, but now a feedback mechanism of my feeling alerts me. I remember to listen and with that deeper listening comes deeper insight. I'm still learning to listen at a deeper and deeper level, I don't think that will ever end.

Do you prepare for a client session and if so, how?

I like to come to an agreement with the client about what they are hoping to gain from our conversations. And that's how

I see it, we are having a conversation. I like to get that agreement and a sense of rapport and trust with each other. The client's goals become part of my reflection, it's in the back of my mind, my sense of that person and of what they are asking. These thoughts guide me, but I always start with nothing on the table. I am open to seeing what shows up.

I don't have any rules, it's what occurs to me. I listen to that inner guidance. Something might occur to me that I'd really like to know about, that I remembered from our last conversation. I might ask about it. I want to show up open to see what this moment calls for because like I said, the guide isn't me, it's that wisdom within us all.

What's your intention with a client, if any? Are you trying to get them to see anything?

I think this has been a big learning for me as a mentor and therapist. I know in my heart of hearts that when people get a deeper insight into the truth of the Principles this will help them on all levels. I think I used to try to push my teaching of the Principles too soon before my client was ready to hear it and before they saw the relevance of listening to what I was sharing.

My intention now is to come into the session with an open mind and to be present in that moment. Part of what I'm listening for is the insights or lack of insights in the client and in myself. Maybe I don't understand the client well enough. Why isn't the client moving forward? What am I missing? I'm listening to see if I can hear what's getting in the way or what would be helpful.

Is there a process to your coaching? Components?

First of all I want to get to know the person and what it is they hope to gain from our conversations. I look for a level of comfort or rapport with the person, that we feel connected. Then I listen. I ask questions that come to my mind, anything I might be curious about. It's an organic process and I don't have a pre-defined strategy.

I show up and listen. Some people just want me to talk and sometimes that's fine. Usually though, I feel like I need to listen before I say much. I need to find out what the client is seeing, what it means to them, and how that's working for them in their life.

Sometimes clients are not looking for anything specific, they want to have a deeper understanding of how the mind works. Perhaps they have been touched previously by this understanding. People know when they have heard something that's true beyond what they have heard before and they want to go deeper.

What happens within you if you get into trouble with a client? What do you do?

I might beat myself up for a while. I'm really good at that! Not for very long though. I might say "Geez, what was I thinking?" I might do a little of that, but then I get curious again. It's that curiosity that puts me into reflection and what it is I need to see. Usually it's that I've gone off on some intellectual explanation versus drawing wisdom out from the client.

Another thing I notice is when I feel a little pressure to help the client or I realise the feeling of rapport and connection is not as solid. I always start with myself though, I ask myself, "What do I need to see here?"

Once in a while I will reach out to the client via an email in between sessions to ask a question or to share a thought. I do what occurs to me and then I learn from that. I feel like I am always a student. I don't own the truth I'm sharing and pointing to, that truth is universal. No one owns it and everyone is it, so to speak. It's discovering that for ourselves then I'm back to the drawing board.

I will also check in with a colleague from time to time and get a little mentoring for myself. The only person I read and listen to, regularly, is Sydney Banks and I have been doing that for 40+ years. I might go for a walk and listen to a Syd recording. His message is so simple, profound and universal it helps clear my mind. I know I need to get back to a place where my mind is free of any insecurity about what I might have done or not done.

Sometimes I realise that I need to refer a client, that we're just not a good fit for whatever the reason. Interestingly, when we have this discussion, whatever wasn't connecting can get cleared up. I don't have an investment one way or the other. Most important to me is that people find what they need and I would never want to get in the way of that. I want to be a caretaker of truth without ego so if we're not a good match, that's okay.

Is problem solving for a client the end of the story? Or do you go further?

I don't tend to think in terms of problem solving. I guess I tend to look at it more as helping people find what they need from inside and whatever issue or problem they have will be answered. There is always an answer.

When people get clarity about the Principles, they often have insights about whatever they sought counselling or coaching for. But that's just the tip of the iceberg because now they are starting to realise that what they learned applies across the board. Instead of being a process of pop up problems – now we're going to solve this problem, now this one – their level of understanding shifts. This shift affects everything in life and brings a different perspective on everything: our parenting, our work, our relationships, our finances, etc.

Is the feeling important for you when working with clients?

When I connect with somebody at a deeper level, soul to soul, there's a feeling to it. It's hard to put a name on it but I know it when I feel it. I am usually able to find this feeling with my clients but sometimes it doesn't happen.

A young man came to see me a few years ago wanting some coaching, a very, very intellectual man with a good heart. He had been in different kinds of therapy so he was used to the analytical, trying to analyse himself, analyse other people. We couldn't get very far because he had such strong beliefs that I was never able to help him get beyond, for whatever reason. Our rapport was okay but it wasn't deep and at some point it didn't make sense to continue. I think it is essential to have the connection because then we can really be a team.

Do you think that has to be a two way street?

That's a good question. It certainly appears that the more open the channel between me and my client, the more possibility that insight will emerge with the wisdom that is needed. But, given the true mentor is the innate wisdom within each of us, I know and have seen clients that appeared closed off hear or see something from within themselves, an insight, a sense or feeling, that helps them find hope and possibly the clarity they are seeking. I always have hope knowing that we can't get away from our true spiritual nature. We can only temporarily lose sight of it. That said, I always look for making a strong connection that we are in it together – a two way street, so to speak.

You always know with kids, teenagers especially, they have no patience for no connection. Some people are very good at acting and so it can be missed. I can think we have a good connection, but something niggles at me especially if I say we have a great connection and the person says, "Ahem, yeah". That's very different from "Ah yes". It's the sincerity that comes from truth.

Could you share a story or stories of what worked well and what didn't and what are the takeaways?

The story about the intellectual young man earlier, I could see he so wanted to live in a different feeling than he was living in and he had so many ideas about that and I was never really able to help him... we didn't click. My takeaway from that encounter was to see that deeper listening might have helped. I think I got caught up in the intellectual conversation and I tried to convince him. That never works.

Another takeaway from my work is that I never know what a client is going to see and I can get surprised. I worked with a woman who had had a lot of therapy in her life. She had beliefs about herself as damaged goods. She questioned herself constantly and believed she could not make wise decisions. She had heard the Principles and been touched by them. I don't remember how she found me.

She was going through a particular bad spell and she was struggling. At the end of one of our sessions I said, in an almost offhand way, something like, "So you fell into the pit, hello, we all fall into the pit and it doesn't matter, it doesn't mean anything, it's a moment in time, ten minutes or a week, it doesn't really matter. We're not going anywhere, the truth sustains us no matter what, whether we reap the benefit of it at the moment or not". What she heard was that the ups and downs don't really matter. It's just the human game of life. Everybody forgets and everybody loses sight of the truth. Her insights helped her go from being destitute to having a home, having a community, and thriving in her life. I never know what is going to strike a chord with clients.

It's not my job to have answers. Syd would say that every human being has the wisdom inside of them, that infinite resource is moulded for each of us in the way that we need it. Good to know that we will forget that too temporarily, but it will always come back at some point. We are spiritual beings living a spiritually created human existence, via Divine Mind, Thought and Consciousness, moment to moment. Every moment is a second chance to see and experience life from a place of inner calm, wellbeing, unconditional love, clarity and wisdom.

Afterword

The Story Behind The Book

I imagine you have had many ideas come to you and ignored them. Then there are those that come back time and time again until one day you say to yourself, "I wonder if this could really happen?" This is exactly what I experienced and how this book came into form.

The idea came to visit me *a lot* until one day I finally took action and decided to contact my long time friend and mentor, Jack Pransky. After all, he is an author of several books and knows something about writing a book. I knew nothing! He was also the first teacher I brought over to Spain, and then many more times over the years.

Jack was kind enough to listen to my idea and immediately said, "Great idea! Better get on it before someone else does!" He said he could even ask his publisher to publish it if I was interested. Wow! I'd never written a book in my life and already the inkling of an offer to publish!

I have to admit it took a while for me to get going. Jack advised me that if you want to get a book written, make it a project, not something you do when you have time. He was right. It wasn't until I made it a priority that I actually began. Then something else became a priority and so the dance continued for over three years, and here we are with a published book!

I spoke to Jack again when I was sure I wanted to devote time to making it happen. I had my list of questions about all things involving book writing and publishing, but most importantly, who are the people to talk to?

This whole book would not be in existence if it wasn't for Sydney Banks' enlightenment experience in 1973 and his never-ending willingness to share what he knew. I was clear that I wanted to interview those who learned directly from him and who presently work with clients. He reeled off a list of names with their email addresses and I scribbled them down furiously. I had never heard of a few of them, which I fully expected hence enlisting the help of Jack.

Next on my to-do list were the all important questions. In my mind it made sense to ask them all the same questions and Jack also helped me put those together. I then invited a group of coaches to submit questions that they would ask if they could. So between Jack, the group and myself, a master list of questions emerged.

I was also aware there would be "in the moment" curiosity, asking questions "off plan," but I wanted to be sure to have some core content, not knowing yet how I would put it all together.

My next step was to send out an invitation to all the people on the list. I was fortunate enough to receive lots of enthusiastic emails saying "Yes" and letting me know it was a great idea.

I sent everyone the questions ahead of time. Some reflected on the questions and some preferred not to look at the questions, but rather see what came to them in the moment. Still others said they hadn't realised there were questions sent to them ahead of time! But they all wanted to go ahead and see what showed up on the call.

Surprisingly to me, when I thought I had finished and sent the final draft out for reviews, I received some very interesting and helpful feedback. I wasn't done at all and neither were the contributors! Once I was clear on my direction I requested a little more input from them.

The chapters materialised because of those who were kind enough to spend time with me to answer my questions. They patiently went through the back and forth of the editing process and gave their approval to the final version.

My Story

It was 2010 and I was looking for some answers to my money problems. I wholeheartedly believed in personal development and had recently completed an NLP course – this serendipitously resulted in me subscribing to Jamie Smart's mailing list. One day, an email landed in my inbox from Jamie with the headline, "If the Secret's So Great Show Me the Money." It piqued my curiosity. *The Secret* had been a popular "Law of Attraction" book and movie around that time and despite my best attempts to use some of the recommended techniques nothing had changed.

Jamie offered the recording of a two day event he had held in London earlier that year. I was intrigued. Could this be the answer I was looking for? I waited patiently for the DVDs to land on my doorstep hoping he would teach me some revolutionary techniques to "show me the money" and relieve my financial stress.

That's not what happened. Not at all. It was so much more than techniques; I heard something that inexplicably touched my soul. I didn't realise this at the time, but with hindsight it's clear to me that's what happened. You might be wondering what I mean by "touched my soul". Have you been moved to tears for no logical reason at all? Or filled up with a beautiful feeling without a logical explanation? As I said, inexplicable. So the best I can do is describe the clues it left behind.

What clearly impacted me was hearing there is only one way we experience life – from the inside-out – 100% of the time, NO exception. That was a massive shift for me. 100% of the time, NO exceptions!

It wasn't that I didn't understand happiness was an inside job – my personal development journey had taught me that much – it was the idea that there was not a single situation in life that could possibly be responsible for my feelings. Including my financial situation. Really? My money stress wasn't because of my financial mess? That was a tall order because it absolutely looked that way.

Jamie was very clear that we should not believe him and he left us with some definite instructions to explore for ourselves. We were to take a look at our own lives over the coming days and see if it was true – asking the question, "Are you feeling your situation or are you feeling your thinking about the situation?"

As any good student would, I did my "homework". I observed my feelings, I questioned whether the situation was directly causing me to feel happy or angry or irritated or frustrated. Was the fact that my partner's socks were on the living room floor AGAIN the cause of my irritation? Yesterday they were on the floor and I wasn't bothered. Last week they were on the floor and I joked about it. Other days I had been more than irritated, downright annoyed and voiced my opinion. Those poor socks on the floor, just doing their thing and me thinking it was his fault for the way I was feeling.

So far, so good. My observation was proving it was indeed a one way system. Then I started to see the implications of my experience of the world only working from the inside-out. What? No longer could I blame anybody else for the way I feel? That felt a bit radical and unfair! It's hard to make a 180 degree turn and live life with a whole different perspective, especially when most of the world believes that life works the other way round.

It felt liberating. No longer would I have to try and change my circumstances or my partner or my kids or my parents in order to feel the way I want to feel! That was absolutely liberating. What, no more controlling to feel okay? Really?

Now, I confess that I'm still in the reforming stages of being a control freak; it hasn't left me completely, but when I notice that I'm doing that "controlling thing" again it's a breath of fresh air. My hands come off the steering wheel and I sit back and relax.

My feelings have zilch to do with what is happening "out there". My feelings have everything to do with what I'm thinking at that moment. Full stop. I can relax and know that when the thinking settles it changes because it always does. It's how the system works.

Over the past eleven years I have repeatedly had that insight! The idea that the outside world causes me to feel a certain way catches me out over and over again. It was my first insight and looks like my forever insight!

Back to my first encounter with Jamie – I said I had been inexplicably touched, but hadn't realised it. If you knew anything about me, you would know I am no fan of repetition. I don't watch the same movie twice, read a book twice, listen to a webinar twice... you get the picture. Yet I found myself attending three more of Jamie's weekend events in London where he pretty much repeated the same message over and over. And I loved it! Now I see I loved the feeling, and my soul had heard Truth. It was like coming home though I hadn't recognised it then.

What I did realise was that I couldn't ignore what I had found. This was life-changing stuff and seemed to me to be the missing piece to so many personal development techniques I had learned to date. I needed to share it.

At the beginning I didn't know how to integrate it into my work with my coaching clients, it felt too ethereal, too formless, so I followed what made sense to me. I shared CDs where others explained it, I interviewed teachers and I even created an annual telesummit to keep spreading the word. Eventually I had other teachers come to Spain and teach on retreats plus speak at the annual Viva Event*, something I co-created with my good friend and colleague, Sue Pankiewicz. I couldn't help myself. I have been moved to keep helping spread the word.

How can you ignore something that has such a profound effect on people's lives?

I have been extremely fortunate to be able to share this understanding and have it be part of my work. And here I am again, doing more of what I love through the generosity of these coaches, therapists and mentors in sharing what they have experienced over the years.

*Viva information can be found at www.thevivaevent.com

Acknowledgements

Creating this book has been way more work than I had anticipated and it definitely took a team to make it to the finish line!

My first thank you goes to Sydney Banks, an ordinary man who had an extraordinary experience and spent the rest of his life sharing what he had realised. Without his willingness to share what he had seen over and over again, the people featured in this book would not have been able to share it with their clients. This understanding has rippled out across the globe and impacted thousands upon thousands of lives. Thank you Syd.

Jamie Smart was the man who first introduced me to the Three Principles and I shall be forever grateful for that. He has a vision of everybody on the planet waking up to their innate capacity for clarity, resilience and wellbeing and continues to spread the word far and wide. Thank you for following your heart, Jamie.

Jamie's transformation was catalysed by his coach and mentor, Michael Neill. Thank you Michael, not only for the absolutely gorgeous foreword you created for this book, but for the prolific creation and inspiration you offer the world through your books, courses, podcasts, trainings and mentoring. You never fail to make me smile through your insightful teachings, colourful stories and brilliant metaphors.

And my friend and mentor, Jack Pransky. Thank you for your encouragement from the first day I shared my idea with you for this book. I was blessed to have you on my team! We have shared some very special trainings together in Spain over seven years with amazing groups of individuals from across the globe. And you have been with me on the journey with the book too. Advising me on who worked directly with Syd, offering ideas for the questions, editing my original introduction and even the offer of introducing me to your publisher. Thank you for your invaluable support Jack, it means so much.

And then there were the intrepid editors who I am honoured to call good friends – Sue Pankiewicz, Sue Lachman, Anne Curtis, Katja Symons and the star player, Carina Loweth, who was with me every step of the way. Thank you all so very, very much for your time and patience in my first endeavour.

My chief proof-reader, Sue Pankiewicz. Thank you my beautiful friend for your ongoing support with this project and many others. And Carina, you were a marvel in the proof-reading department too. Thank you again.

My brother-in-law, Nigel Smith, blew my socks off with his first drafts for the book cover! Wow, his talent and professionalism shone through. Thank you Nige for listening and making the cover an effortless part of the process. Shame we didn't use a piece of your amazing artwork ... maybe another time! View his stunning pieces at www.nigelsmithart.com/

And finally, a huge thank you to the contributors of the book without whom none of this would have been possible. Thank you for your willingness to give of your time and energy through interviews and editing. An idea came into the form because each one of these coaches, therapists and mentors said yes. Thank you Joe Bailey, Dicken Bettinger, Lori Carpenos, Christine Heath, Mark Howard, Annika Hurwitt, Sandy Krot, Gabriela Maldonado-Montano, Ken Manning, Bill Pettit, George Pransky, Jack Pransky, Linda Pransky, Judy Sedgeman and Rita Shuford.

Thank you for your years of dedication to sharing the Three Principles and enabling transformation to take place for your countless clients. Your willingness to share with me your thoughts, experiences, personal points of view and ways of working, has provided an invaluable resource for coaches, therapists and counsellors across the globe for years to come. Who knows how many more lives will be transformed?

Thank you from the bottom of my heart.

A Juicy List of Resources for You

If you would like to find out more about the contributors, please use the contact details below. Many of them have authored their own books, offer educational programmes, produce videos and/or podcasts.

Annika Hurwitt PhD
http://annikahurwitt.com/

Dr William F Pettit Jr MD and Retired Psychiatrist
http://www.thedrspettit.com/

Christine Heath LMFT, MAC
https://www.hawaiicounselingandeducationcenter.com/

Dicken Bettinger EdD and Retired Psychologist
http://www.3principlesmentoring.com

Gabriela Maldonado-Montano
@gabrielayourcoach @gabrielatucoach on Facebook and Instagram

George Pransky PhD
http://www.pranskyandassociates.com

Jack Pransky PhD
https://insideoutunderstanding.com/

Joseph Bailey MA, LP
http://www.joebaileyandassociates.com

Judith Sedgeman EdD
https://three-principles.com/

Ken Manning PhD
http://www.insightprinciplesinstitute.com

Linda Pransky
http://www.pranskyandassociates.com

Lori Carpenos LMFT
http://www.3principlestherapy.com/

Mark Howard PhD
http://www.drmarkhoward.com

Rita Shuford PhD
http://www.threeprincipleshawaii.com

Sandra Krot
http://www.insightprinciples.com/

To find out more about Sydney Banks and the resources he created, please visit:
www.sydneybanks.com
www.sydneybanks.org

About the Author

In 2010 Sheela Masand was introduced to a psycho-spiritual understanding called The Three Principles discovered by Sydney Banks, also referred to as the inside-out understanding. She didn't know it then, but her life was to be infused with its unique and undeniable transformative magic. Her coaching business slowly transformed in the same way – she couldn't help but share the Principles in all her work.

There was a natural pull for her to continue her own exploration of how life works from the inside-out and to share that with others, plus support those who were sharing too. This led to the creation and organisation of annual events, retreats and programmes, both in-person and online. She also created and hosted an annual telesummit for three consecutive years in collaboration with a non-profit organisation.

Her love of all things business from her past life as an importer of food and drink, and being a forever-student of the Principles gives her an effective springboard and solid ground from which to help her coaching clients. Not only do they grow their businesses and practices, but they deepen their own grounding as they wake up to the infinite potential that lies within and realise the peace that is their true nature.

Sheela was born and raised in England, but found herself yearning to travel. At some point she landed in Spain, fell in love, married, and had two beautiful daughters. She continues to enjoy living on the Costa Blanca, famed for its 320 days of sunshine per year.

You can find out more about Sheela and her work at: www.sheelamasand.com

Thank You

If you enjoyed this book, I would be extremely grateful if you'd leave a brief review at the store you purchased from. Book reviews can spread the word and help readers find the best book for them.

You will find links to the main stores for your convenience here: http://insideouttransformation.org

Thank you.

Printed in Great Britain
by Amazon

87313797R00146